Children in Tax Planning

Children in Tax Planning

Peter White LLM
Solicitor

Oyez Publishing Ltd

Oyez Publishing Limited
Norwich House, 11/13 Norwich Street,
London EC4A 1AB

ISBN 0 85120 513 5

First published 1980

Printed and bound in Great Britain by
Redwood Burn Limited
Trowbridge & Esher

Contents

INTRODUCTION

Children may not always sweeten the labours of their parents but most parents will feel a strong obligation to apply at least some of the rewards of those labours for the benefit of their offspring. While the child is young, day to day living expenses must be met, holidays must be paid for, clothes and toys have to be bought and perhaps school fees have to be paid. As the child grows up, a parent's financial outlay increases; a car or motorbike may be supplied, the wedding and the child's first house may well require considerable funds. When the child reaches full maturity (whenever that may happen – sometimes never) it may be appropriate to pass him an interest in the family business or other substantial capital assets. Eventually, when the parents die, property will pass to the child or his issue.

Sound tax planning is crucial throughout. With income tax and capital transfer tax at rates up to 75 per cent and capital gains tax at 30 per cent, vast sums can be gained or lost by adopting different courses of action for the same transfer of funds – for example, a misdirected pension fund benefit can substantially increase the capital transfer tax burden.

This book examines the tax planning opportunities which a parent has when providing financial benefits for his children and their issue. The opportunities exist throughout the parent's lifetime and on his death and apply regardless of the age of the child. The book also shows the opportunities available for grandparents and others to benefit the child.

The expression "child" is often assumed to be synonymous with minority. In ordinary English usage, the expression seems to mean someone under the age of 16 or 17, but it can also mean the issue of the first generation – sons and daughters as opposed to grandchildren. In this book, references to children take the latter meaning and, unless otherwise indicated, do not imply an age limitation. A child can be 5 or 50 years old.

No other exposition exists which deals solely with the tax planning opportunities for children; this book is designed to fill that important gap.

ABBREVIATIONS

AEA 1925	Administration of Estates Act 1925
CGTA 1979	Capital Gains Tax Act 1979
FA	Finance Act
ICTA 1970	Income and Corporation Taxes Act 1970
MCA 1973	Matrimonial Causes Act 1973

Table of Statutes

Table of Cases

Chapter 1

CHILDREN, MINORITY AND TAXATION

1.01 The minor child as a separate taxable unit

A child is a potential taxpayer in his own right from the day he first appears in this world and, generally speaking, extreme youth and minority do not affect his capacity to pay tax and to claim the relevant exemptions and reliefs. It is this separate capacity for taxation that makes tax planning for children possible, so it is worth looking at it in more detail.

Residence and ordinary residence

Like any other taxpayer, a minor child's residence and ordinary residence are central in the determination of his various tax liabilities. These are a question of fact and both require some measure of physical presence in the United Kingdom although, in the case of ordinary residence, not necessarily in the particular tax year. Generally, if a child is living with his parents, his residence and ordinary residence will be the same as theirs, but not always. In *Miesegaes* v *IRC* (1957) 37 TC 493 a boy attending boarding school in the United Kingdom was held to be ordinarily resident here, although he spent his holidays with his Dutch father who was resident in Switzerland.

Domicile

The Revenue view on domicile is that, broadly speaking, a person is domiciled in the country in which he has his permanent home. Domicile is distinct from nationality or residence. At birth, a child acquires a domicile of origin – generally that of his father; until he reaches the age of sixteen or earlier marries, he is incapable of having a separate domicile, so his domicile will change with that of his father or whoever his domicile is dependent upon. Thereafter a child is capable of having a separate domicile (DMPA 1973, s 3(1)).

Income Tax

The income tax liability of a minor child is computed in the same way as for adults. He has a single person's relief of £1,375 for the tax year 1980/81 (or, if married, a married man's relief of £2,145) and will pay tax on his taxable income at progressive rates, starting at 30 per cent on the first £11,250 and rising to 60 per cent on the excess over £27,750. The additional rate of tax at 15 per cent is leviable on his investment income over £5,500.

A child's personal relief is a valuable asset which is wasted more often than not; unfortunately, parents who wish to alienate income to their children to make use of the relief have to contend with ICTA 1970, s 437 (see p 34) which makes ineffective for income tax purposes any settlement, trust, covenant, agreement, arrangement or transfer of assets by the settlor for the benefit of his infant unmarried children. However, grandparents and others can effectively alienate their income to the children to use up the personal relief (see Chapter 4), and this is an opportunity which should be used.

A child of tender years may not qualify for life assurance relief (see p 63).

Capital gains tax

A minor child is a separate taxable individual for capital gains tax. He is generally capable of holding personal property (see 1.04 below) but not of dealing effectively with it. If he does make a disposal, it may well be voidable but it is nevertheless liable to capital gains tax. He is eligible for the £3,000 annual exemption (FA 1980, s 77) and, subject to other exemptions, will pay tax at 30 per cent on the balance of his chargeable gains.

Usually property will be held for a minor child by adults, either as bare trustees or as trustees of a settlement for the benefit of the child. A bare trust is not a settlement for capital gains tax even though the beneficiary is a minor (CGTA 1979, s 46), and the acts of the trustees are deemed to be those of the beneficiary; this is despite the fact that TA 1925, s 31 (see p 39) empowers the trustee to accumulate income. If the minor has any interest other than an absolute interest, for example if he has a life interest or a contingent interest, eg requiring him to attain a specified age such as 21, the property will be settled property for capital gains tax and the normal settlement rules will apply. These are dealt with in Chapter 3.

Capital transfer tax

Again, a minor child is a separate taxable person. He has all the capital transfer tax exemptions and reliefs and his chargeable transfers are taxed normally, eg the first £50,000 of chargeable transfers are taxed at a nil rate. However, a minor cannot make a gift which is binding on him and any gift which he does make will be voidable until a reasonable time after he attains full age. By FA 1976, s 88 if a transaction is avoided the capital transfer tax paid is refunded and the amount of the gift is expunged from the donor's cumulation. Where the property of a minor child is held for him by adults the trusts will almost always be an accumulation and maintenance settlement if TA 1925, s 31 applies, whether or not the child's interest is absolute, so no adverse capital transfer tax consequences will arise (see Chapter 3).

Development land tax

Where, exceptionally, a minor disposes of an interest in land (ie where it is held by others for him absolutely), if development land tax is chargeable, he will be treated in the same way as any other taxpayer. As will be seen below (1.04) it will be rare for a minor to have an interest in land.

Usually a minor's interest will be under a settlement and the charge will arise to the trustees.

1.02 Parent and child

The relationship of parent and child gives rise to certain tax consequences. One of the more adverse results of it arose briefly during the tax years 1969/70 to 1971/72 when the investment income of a minor child was aggregated with that of his parent. The rule was abolished for the tax year 1972/73 onwards and no longer exists. A second adverse result is the income tax anti-avoidance provisions in ICTA 1970, s 437. This is dealt with in Chapter 2 and Chapter 3. The other consequences are described below.

Income tax relief for children

A parent may qualify for two different personal reliefs if he has a child.

CHILD RELIEF

From the tax year 1979/80 onwards child relief was replaced in most cases by child benefit (see below), but in two cases it may still be claimed by a parent who can show that he has a child living at any time in the tax year or that he has custody of and maintains, at his own expense, any other child. Custody here means responsibility for the child's upbringing and does not necessarily mean that the child lives with the taxpayer. The two cases in which the relief is still available are:

(*a*) on 31 December 1976 the child was (generally) over nineteen and was and still is following a full time course at university, college, school or other educational establishment; and

(*b*) the child is under nineteen at the end of the tax year, lives outside the United Kingdom (but not in certain stipulated countries, eg Australia, Jersey and Spain) and no child benefit is payable in respect of him.

The amount of the relief varies from £300 to £365, depending on the age of the child, and is being phased out in the case of overseas children from the tax year 1981/82 onwards. Child relief for students will phase itself out as the children concerned qualify.

There are provisions reducing the relief if the child has income over a specified amount.

ADDITIONAL CHILD RELIEF

This is an important relief for single parent families and its amount, £770, is designed to make up the parent's single person's relief to the amount of the married man's relief. A parent will qualify for this relief if he can show that he has resident with him for at least part of the tax year a child who is under sixteen at the start of the tax year or, if over sixteen, is attending full time instruction at university, college, school or other educational establishment or undergoing full time training for at least 2 years for a trade, profession or vocation. Unless the child is the claimant's child (including illegitimate, adopted, legitimated or stepchild) the child must be under eighteen at the start of the tax year and be maintained for the whole or part of that year by the claimant at his own expense.

No relief is given to a person entitled to married man's relief unless his wife is totally incapacitated by physical or mental infirmity throughout the tax year. Nor is relief given to either spouse where there has been an election for separate taxation for the tax year. It will be claimable, however, on separation or divorce.

An individual can only qualify for one relief, regardless of the number of children he has resident with him. If two or more individuals are entitled to the relief in respect of the same child it is apportioned between them as they agree or, failing agreement, in proportion to the length of the period for which the child is resident with them respectively in the tax year. Thus, where spouses are separated or divorced and there are two children of the family, it should always be possible to ensure that both spouses obtain additional child relief in full, each claiming in respect of a different child. Residence for a relatively short period should suffice, eg during school holidays. Both spouses would probably qualify in respect of each child but they can agree that each can claim a full relief for one child. An unmarried couple living together with two children can therefore claim £770 each.

Should a child be legitimate or illegitimate?

We are here concerned only with the tax aspects of this question. If an unmarried couple have children, there are three points which can make it more advantageous to stay single rather than to get married and legitimate the children.

(*a*) If there are two children, the couple can each claim additional child relief of £770, each thus achieving a personal relief of £2,145, equivalent to the married man's relief. This is £770 more than a married couple can achieve in the same circumstances.

(*b*) If the woman has investment income, it will be aggregated with the man's income if they marry while they co-habit, and there is no election to disaggregate it. This can substantially increase the husband's top rate of tax bill. If they do not marry her investment income remains hers for income tax purposes.

(*c*) If one of the unmarried couple, eg the woman, has insufficient income to make use of her personal reliefs, the man can make a covenant in her favour; this gives him basic rate tax relief and she can then claim back the tax credit by setting off her unused personal relief against the receipt. If they were married and living together, a covenant by one party to the other would have no tax effect whatever – being investment income, the covenanted payment would be treated as that of the husband in any event; the only personal relief he is allowed for his wife is in respect of her earned income.

Child benefit

The Child Benefit Act 1975 has introduced a system of non-taxable child benefits. This has replaced family allowances (which were taxable) and child relief. The benefits are payable in respect of a qualifying child, usually to the mother, and the current benefit rate is £4.00 per week for each child (£4.75 per week from 24 November 1980). To qualify a child must be under sixteen, or over sixteen but under nineteen and undergoing full time advanced education.

Capital transfer tax – dispositions for the maintenance of the family

The parent/child relationship enables the parent to make dispositions for the maintenance, education or training of the child without liability to capital transfer tax. This is dealt with on p 26.

1.03 Assessment and repayment claims

By TMA 1970, s 118(1) a minor is classified as an incapacitated person and as a result his trustee, guardian or tutor, amongst others, can be assessed under TMA 1970, s 72(1) for tax on his behalf. As a matter of practice, it will usually be the minor's parents who are assessed, but there is nothing to prevent the Revenue from making an assessment on the minor direct, as in *R* v *Newmarket IT Comrs* [1916] 1 KB 788.

If the minor is entitled to a repayment of tax, eg as a result of personal reliefs or where the income is accumulation and maintenance trust income carrying a tax credit of 45 per cent and the minor has income under £5,500, a claim will be made on his behalf by his parent or guardian to whom the repayment will be made.

1.04 Minority and the law

Tax planning may require a consideration of whether a minor child should hold property or exercise certain powers personally. It is usually far more sensible to have the property held or powers exercised by a parent or by trustees, although it may not always be practicable, eg in a partnership of which the minor is a member. Nevertheless, the following brief resumé of the law relating to the capacity of a minor should persuade the tax planner to avoid giving a minor personal power over any property.

Contracts

VALID CONTRACTS

In two cases, contracts made by a minor are valid and binding on him, and he can be sued on them. They are:

(*a*) contracts for necessaries, ie goods suitable to the

condition in life of the minor and to his actual requirements at the time of sale and delivery; and
(*b*) contracts of employment if, taken as a whole, they are for his benefit.

VOIDABLE CONTRACTS

A minor may repudiate the following contracts before attaining majority or within a reasonable time thereafter:

(*a*) contracts concerning land;
(*b*) contracts to subscribe for, or buy, company shares;
(*c*) partnership contracts; and
(*d*) marriage settlements.

VOID CONTRACTS

Under the Infants' Relief Act 1874 all contracts by minors for the repayment of money or for goods supplied (other than necessaries) and all accounts stated are said to be "absolutely void". The meaning of this expression still causes considerable difficulty. The answer is to give a wide berth to contracts with minors.

Torts

A minor is just as liable for his torts as an adult, but he is not liable if the effect would be to enforce indirectly a contract which is not binding on him.

Wills

A minor cannot make a Will (Wills Act 1837, s 7) unless he is a soldier on actual military service, or a mariner or seaman at sea, in which case he may make a privileged will (Wills Act 1837, s 11 and Wills (Soldiers and Sailors) Act 1918, s 1).

Land

A minor can never hold a legal estate in land (LPA 1925, s1(6)). A conveyance of land to him operates as an agreement to settle the land in his favour and if he then dies before reaching majority, or earlier marrying, the property reverts to the settlor according to AEA 1925, s 51(3)).

A conveyance by a minor is voidable by the infant before attaining majority or within a reasonable time thereafter.

Partnerships

A partnership contract is, as mentioned above, voidable by a minor.

Shares

A minor may become a member of a company, but he may avoid the allotment or transfer of shares to him before attaining majority or within a reasonable time thereafter. A company can refuse to register a transfer to a minor. While the minor is a member, until repudiation, he is contractually bound by the Memorandum and Articles of Association and can vote.

Directorships

A person is not disqualified from appointment as a director merely because he is a minor, subject to the Articles of Association of the company.

Chapter 2

CAPITAL TRANSFER TAX PLANNING FOR CHILDREN

2.01 Outright gifts

Generally

Outright gifts to or for the benefit of a child are usually only suitable if the child is of mature years or if the donor or someone acting for him can keep control over the gifted property. It is rarely appropriate to make substantial gifts outright to a young child. Where there is doubt about the expediency of an outright gift, it may be that a settlement would be more appropriate and this topic is dealt with in Chapter 3. Formal settlements are, however, expensive to set up and run and in many cases the donor may prefer to make an outright gift and risk the consequences rather than to go through the rigmarole of creating a settlement. For example, it would be ridiculous formally to settle a £250 gift on a 6 year old child; either the money should be given to the child's parents for them to invest for the child, or if the donor is the parent, the money should be invested for the child by the donor. On the other hand, a gift of shares in a private company or a cash gift of £250,000 should be settled on fairly restrictive terms, using an accumulation and maintenance settlement.

Income tax problems

One problem which is common both to outright and settled gifts to a child is the income tax anti-avoidance provision, ICTA 1970, s 437. This is dealt with in Chapter 3 in its application to settled property but its effect on outright gifts must be considered here.

ICTA 1970, s 437 provides that income from a settlement is treated as that of the settlor for all income tax purposes if the income is or may become payable to the infant unmarried child of the settlor. The term "settlement" is defined by ICTA 1970, s 444(2) and includes any disposition, trust, covenant, agreement, arrangement or transfer of assets. In *Thomas* v *Marshall* [1953] AC 543 a father made outright cash gifts to his infant unmarried children and paid the cash into Post Office Savings Bank accounts in their name, and bought them Defence Bonds. It was held that these transactions were settlements within ICTA 1970, s 437 and that the income from the investments should be treated as that of the father. Thus outright gifts are within ICTA 1970, s 437.

There are two main exceptions to ICTA 1970, s 437. The first is that it does not apply to income accumulated in an irrevocable settlement of capital (see p 34). The second is that the section is ignored if the aggregate of all income arising from ICTA 1970, s 437 settlements on each child, does not exceed £5 each tax year; the scope for operating within this is somewhat limited.

Solution to the income tax problem

The solution to the ICTA 1970, s 437 problem is simple. If it is desired to make an outright gift to an infant unmarried child of the donor, the gift should be of non-income producing property, eg premium bonds, a stamp collection and in some cases, private company shares. If income producing assets are to be given, an irrevocable settlement of capital must be used and which should also be an accumulation and maintenance settlement.

Gifts to adult children and those to married minor children are not within ICTA 1970, s 437.

2.02 When should the gift be made?

This is a constant problem and there are no hard and fast rules. The time when a gift should be made depends on a number of factors which may influence the donor to make the gift immediately, or he may wait to make the gift later during his lifetime; alternatively he may choose to make the gift by Will to take effect on his death. The factors which every donor should take into account are:

Can you afford it?

A surprising number of parents are happy to give away to their children large chunks of their fortune, leaving themselves with inadequate resources for later life. Tax planning must always be secondary to the normal requirements of life and unless the donor is satisfied that he and his dependants will be able to manage adequately with his remaining resources for the rest of their lives, the gift should be reduced or not made at all.

Will the burden of capital taxation change?

It is usually reckoned that unless there is likely to be a major review of capital taxation in the foreseeable future, possible changes in the system or rates of capital taxation should be ignored; to do otherwise would be to indulge in speculation. If the burden is likely to be eased, it may be advisable to wait; those who made substantial gifts before the 1980 Budget are now regretting the fact that they did not wait to take advantage of the new capital gains tax gift relief and the amelioration in the capital transfer tax burden following the hoisting of the nil rate band from £25,000 to £50,000.

The Conservative Government have promised a review of capital taxation within the next year and all other things being equal, a gift which will attract a significant amount of capital taxation now, should wait until the results of the review are known.

The possibility of a "Wealth Tax" must never be forgotten, even though the introduction of such a tax is only likely on a change of Government.

Fiscal drag

The rates of capital transfer tax have been changed twice since 1974 but, except in the case of smaller estates, these changes have not kept pace with inflation. Capital gains tax feeds on inflation and as time marches on, the burden increases, although, where small amounts are involved, the exemption for the first £3,000 of chargeable gains each tax year, introduced by the FA 1980, s 77, does provide a significant relief. Overall, large gifts should be made sooner rather than later to avoid the worst effects of fiscal drag.

Probable fluctuations in the value of the gifted asset

The effect of fiscal drag is aggravated if the value of the asset to be given away is likely to increase more rapidly than the rate of inflation. Clearly, if this is the case, it becomes important to give away the asset as soon as possible to minimise the capital tax burden. Equally, if the value of an asset is unlikely to increase as fast as the rate of inflation and in particular if the value of the asset is likely to decrease, it is usually cheaper to wait.

Capital transfer tax: lifetime rates now or higher rates later?

On transfers of value up to a cumulative total of £110,000, capital transfer tax at the lifetime rates is exactly half that charged at the higher rates applicable to death and to transfers made within three years of death. Up to £310,000, the lifetime rates are lower. Thereafter they are the same. Since no-one can predict their own date of death, this difference in rates may influence donors to give now rather than later. Even if it is thought likely that the donor will die within 3 years after making the gift, the gift itself will still be cheaper if it is made during the donor's lifetime rather than on his death, although the overall burden of capital transfer tax on the gift and on the estate will be the same. The following example illustrates these points.

Example 1

A, a widower, has an estate of £500,000. Having made no previous chargeable transfers, he gives £250,000 to one of his two sons and the son bears the capital transfer tax. A dies 4 years later, leaving the remainder of his estate to his other son:

	CTT	*Net value*
Lifetime gift of £250,000 to son, taxed at lifetime rates	£ 69,000	£181,000
Estate on death of £250,000	£150,000	£100,000
	£219,000	£281,000

If A had died within 3 years of the lifetime gift, the figures would be:

Lifetime gift of £250,000 taxed at the higher rates	£104,000	£146,000
Estate on death of £250,000	£150,000	£100,000
	£254,000	£246,000

If A had made no lifetime gift, but had divided his £500,000 equally between his two sons on death, each son would have borne the £254,000 tax bill equally:

Received by first son	£127,000	£123,000
Received by second son	£127,000	£123,000
	£254,000	£246,000

The lifetime gift is thus cheaper, regardless of when the donor dies, but the existence of the lifetime gift does make the estate passing on death bear a proportionately greater capital transfer tax burden. From the point of view of the second son, the lifetime gift reduces his benefit on death and destroys equality between offspring (see p 20).

A disadvantage of making lifetime gifts is that the capital transfer tax is immediately payable and it may be that the loss of the use of the money outweighs the advantage of the lifetime rates of tax.

Example 2

A has an estate of £500,000 and wishes to give B £250,000. He can either do so now or wait till he dies (1990).

	CTT	*Net gift*
Give £250,000 now		
Gift of £250,000	£ 69,000	£181,000
Estate on death £250,000	£150,000	£100,000
	£219,000	£281,000
Gifts by Will in 1990		
Gift of £250,000	£127,000	£123,000
Residue of £250,000	£127,000	£123,000
	£254,000	£246,000

By making the gift now, A lost the use of £69,000 for 10 years, but saved £35,000, assuming the rates of capital transfer tax do not change in the meanwhile – and ignoring inflation! If the lost £69,000 had been invested by A at, eg 5 per cent net of income tax, simple interest over 10 years would produce £34,500, virtually eliminating the capital transfer tax saving.

Clearly inflation, changes in the capital transfer tax rates and capital gains tax (see below) play an important part in this decision but the example illustrates the point that the real tax saving on a lifetime gift my not be so great as imagined.

The £50,000 nil rate

No capital transfer tax liability is incurred to the extent that the value transferred by lifetime chargeable transfers do not exceed £50,000; they are taxed at a nil rate. If this applies, a gift now will not be disadvantageous, except to the extent that, as illustrated on the previous page, a gift of part of an estate during the donor's lifetime makes the remainder of his estate on death proportionately more expensive.

Capital gains tax

As the law now stands, capital gains tax is not payable on death when there is a tax free uplift in base value, so that beneficiaries are deemed to acquire the inherited assets at market value at the date of death. A lifetime gift, on the other hand, is treated as being made at market value and capital gains tax at 30 per cent is leviable (subject to exemptions) unless both donor and donee are individuals and elect to hold-over the chargeable gain until the donee makes a chargeable disposal of the asset (FA 1980, s 79). Even if this hold-over is used (and it is not available on gifts into settlement) the potential capital gains tax liability can be a substantial disincentive to lifetime transfers and is a factor which may influence donors to make the gift on death. However, if the asset is to be retained by the donee throughout his lifetime so that the potential charge will never be realised, since FA 1980 the capital gains tax implications have become less onerous for a lifetime gift.

Making use of the lifetime exemptions

Many of the capital transfer tax exemptions apply to lifetime transfers only, eg the £2,000 exemption, the £250 exemption, the exemption for normal expenditure out of income and gifts in consideration of marriage. It is always advisable to make use of these exemptions, if possible.

Lifetime gift to infant unmarried child of donor

A lifetime gift to an infant unmarried child of the donor may fall foul of ICTA 1970, s 437 whereas the section does not apply if the donor has died, so a gift on death may be more appropriate.

Conclusions

A general guide as to when to make a gift is, first, that it is better to give sooner than later if:

(*a*) the gifted property is likely to increase rapidly in value;

(*b*) to make use of the lifetime exemptions, and possibly the first £50,000 transfers taxed at a nil rate of capital transfer tax.

On the other hand, a gift may have to be postponed if:

(*a*) capital gains tax is a problem;

(*b*) the gift is likely to decrease in value.

2.03 What form should the gift take: property or cash?

Assuming that the gift is to be made during the donor's lifetime, the considerations in deciding whether a gift should be of property or cash include:

Tax by instalments

On lifetime transfers capital transfer tax is payable by eight yearly or sixteen half yearly instalments on certain types of property, but only if the donee bears the tax. This relief is given by FA 1975, Sched 4 to:

(*a*) land;

(*b*) shares and securities of a company which gave the donor control immediately before the transfer;

(*c*) other shares and securities if not quoted and:

(i) the Board of Inland Revenue are satisfied that tax cannot be paid at once without hardship; or

(ii) not less than 20 per cent of the tax payable by the donee is attributable to tax on the shares or securities and to other assets upon which tax is payable by instalments;

(*d*) other shares if not quoted and worth over £5,000, if they form not less than a 10 per cent holding:
(*e*) businesses and interests in businesses;
(*f*) in certain cases timber.

Interest runs on outstanding tax (at 12 per cent on lifetime transfers) but no interest is charged on tax due in respect of property in (*b*)–(*f*) (above), provided the instalments are kept up to date. The first instalment is payable when tax is normally due and payable (see FA 1975, Sched 4, para 12). If cash is given, the instalment option is never available.

Relief on death within 3 years

By FA 1976, s 99, if the donor dies within 3 years of making a gift and the property the subject of the gift is worth less than it was at the time of the gift, the extra capital transfer tax which is payable (see p 14) is calculated by reference to the reduced value. This would not apply if a cash gift had been made instead.

Capital gains tax

If cash is given, capital gains tax will be payable only if the donor has to sell property to realise the cash. If instead of selling the property to produce the cash, the property itself is given, the capital gains tax liability on the gift can be held over if both donor and donee so elect. Like capital transfer tax, capital gains tax can sometimes be paid by instalments (CGTA 1979, s 8, see above).

Valuation

The valuation of property is a matter of negotiation with the Inland Revenue and it may be possible to negotiate a low value particularly if the donor has used the asset. Thus, if the donor wishes the donee to have an expensive yacht, it may be cheaper for the donor to buy it, use it and then give it to the donee rather than for the donor to give the cash to the donee to enable him to buy it himself.

For share valuations, see p 97 *et seq*.

2.04 Who pays the capital transfer tax?

Grossing-up

It is often said that the donee should pay the capital transfer tax on lifetime transfers because it avoids grossing-up. This is an elementary misconception of grossing-up. The amount of capital transfer tax, and thus the amount of the value transferred by a chargeable transfer, depends solely on the amount the donee ends up with after capital transfer tax is paid.

Example 1

A has made previous lifetime chargeable transfers of £70,000, so his next rate band is 20 per cent. He wishes to give B £8,000 and he has no exemptions available to set off against the gift. A has three choices: first, that he should bear the tax; second, that B should bear the tax; third, that B should bear the tax but that he should be given enough for him to end up with £8,000 after paying the tax:

First choice

A gives £8,000 to B and A pays the tax. The £8,000 must be grossed-up at 20 per cent to determine the amount which after deduction of tax at 20 per cent produces £8,000. The gross is £10,000. This is the value transferred and will be cumulated to calculate the rate on subsequent chargeable transfers by A. B receives £8,000.

Second choice

A gives £8,000 to B and B pays the tax. The tax is 20 per cent of £8,000, ie £1,600. No grossing-up is necessary because A's loss is only £8,000. The tax burden is reduced, the chargeable transfer is £8,000 and this is the amount to be taken into account in A's cumulation. The point is that B ends up with £6,400 only. So it is reasonable to expect the tax burden to be lower.

Third choice

A wishes B to bear tax, but he wants B to end up with £8,000. He must, therefore, give B the sum which after paying tax out of it at 20 per cent leaves £8,000. That sum is £10,000. This is the value transferred and the tax bill is £2,000. B ends up with exactly the same as in the first case and it has made no difference who pays the tax if the donee, B, is to end up with the same amount.

The principle illustrated in Example 1, is exactly the same for gifts of property.

Example 2

A farm worth £500,000 is to be given away; with 50 per cent agricultural relief, the value of the farm is £250,000. If the donor pays tax, grossing-up is necessary and the tax payable will be £163,750 (the gross gift being £413,750). If the donee pays tax, the tax will be £69,000, the gross gift being £250,000. Much less tax is paid but the donee ends up with £181,000 instead of £250,000.

Tax by instalments

On lifetime gifts, capital transfer tax is payable by instalments on certain assets (see 2.03) only if the donee pays the tax. If this applies, it is sensible to give the donee sufficient assets to enable him to meet the tax.

2.05 Equality between offspring

Because each chargeable transfer must be cumulated with earlier chargeable transfers to calculate the rates of capital transfer tax applicable to a gift, and because of the progressive rates of capital transfer tax, the capital transfer tax burden on gifts increases as more gifts are made, and later gifts, especially those made on death or within 3 years of death, are more expensive than earlier gifts. This can produce inequality between donees, the recipients of later gifts ending up with less than the recipients of earlier gifts (for an example of this, see p 15).

To maintain equality between donees, there are two alternatives:

(*a*) later gifts must be increased to ensure that what is left after tax is the same as that left in the donee's hands after tax on earlier gifts; or

(*b*) gifts should be made on the same day, when the capital transfer tax rates and exemptions will be apportioned between the gifts rateably according to value.

2.06 Lease and reversion schemes

One way to minimise the capital transfer tax burden on gifts to children is to depress the value of the property to be handed over. A popular way of doing this is by way of a lease and reversion scheme.

The problems

All lease and reversion schemes rely on the fact that if a lease is granted out of freehold property, the aggregate value of the lease and the freehold reversion is substantially less than the value of the unencumbered freehold.

The steps in such a scheme are:

(*a*) the donor parent grants to the donee child a lease of the property at a full market rent and on commercial terms;

(*b*) over 3 years later, the parent sells or gives the reversion to the child.

The associated operations provisions in FA 1975, s 44 do not apply because FA 1975, s 44(2) stipulates that the granting of a lease for full consideration in money or money's worth shall not be taken to be associated with any operation effected more than 3 years later.

The problem is that there is no doubt that when the lease is granted to the child, the parent's estate is substantially reduced. If it were not, there would be little point in doing the scheme. It is argued that the non-gratuitous exemption under FA 1975, s 20(4) applies, but it is submitted that the Inland Revenue is unlikely to be impressed with this argument since, for FA 1975, s 20(4) to apply, it must be shown:

(*a*) that the transaction was at arm's length or on arm's length terms; and

(*b*) that there was no gratuitous intent involved.

Why does the parent enter into the transaction except to benefit the child gratuitously? Capital transfer tax will therefore be payable on the grant of the lease and FA 1975, s 20(4) will not apply. If subsequently the reversion is given (rather than sold) to the child, capital transfer tax will again become payable.

A solution

It is possible to concoct a somewhat involved scheme to avoid the problem. It works as follows:

(*a*) a charitable settlement is created by the parent and registered with the Charity Commission;

(*b*) the freehold reversion is sold to the charity at full market value, reserving to the parent a lease at full market rent. The charity obtains the purchase price by borrowing;

(*c*) the lease and reversion are related property (FA 1975, Sched 10, para 7) and continue to be related until 5 years after the charity relinquishes ownership of the reversion. This means that the value of each of the lease and the reversion is treated as a proportion of the value of the unencumbered freehold. This mitigates the parents' loss on the sale of the reversion when the freehold is divided into two estates, but what loss there is is covered by the charity exemption in FA 1975, Sched 6, para 10. No capital transfer tax is payable on the sale of the reversion, therefore, and no reliance need be placed on FA 1975, s 20(4);

(*d*) over 3 years later, the charity sells the reversion to the child for full market value. The associated operations provisions do not apply (FA 1975, s 44(2)) but the related property provisions continue to apply for another 5 years. The price the charity receives is less than the capital transfer tax related property valuation of the reversion, but no capital transfer tax is payable under the charitable trust exemption (FA 1975, Sched 5, para 20);

(*e*) 5 years later the parent can sell or give the lease to the child. The related property provisions no longer apply and the measure of loss to the parent's estate is simply the value of the lease.

The disadvantage of this scheme is that it takes 8 years to carry out!

2.07 Making the most of the exemptions

Channelling

DOUBLING THE EXEMPTIONS

Both spouses have a full set of capital transfer tax exemptions and reliefs so that, for example, each can give away £2,000 each tax year without liability. It may be the case that one spouse has insufficient resources to make use of the available exemptions and the other may wish to provide the first with funds to enable him or her to do so. This is known as channelling and it is doubtful to what extent the associated operations provisions apply. FA 1975, s 44(1) indicates that a channelled gift is to be treated as a gift by the original donor to the ultimate beneficiary.

Joel Barnett, then Chief Secretary to the Treasury said in the House of Commons on 10 March 1975:

"It is reasonable for a husband to share capital with his wife when she has no means of her own. If she chooses to make gifts out of the money received from her husband, there would be no question of using the associated operations provisions . . . but in a blatant case where a transfer by a husband to a wife is made on condition that the wife should at once use the money in making gifts to others, a charge might arise under the clause."

So, provided there is no obligation on the recipient spouse to pass on the property, channelling should work. It remains to be seen what the Inland Revenue practice will be, but when channelling it would be sensible to keep the two steps separate and distinct.

FIANCÉE CHANNELLING

It has been claimed that a father can pass his fortune to his son by marrying the son's fiancée. Father then dies leaving all his property to his widow, the transfer being exempt under the spouse exemption. Son then marries the widow who gives him all the inherited property. Unfortunately, this scheme does not work. A son cannot by law marry his father's widow, so the second transfer would always be chargeable. However, the scheme could work with a more distant relationship than that of father and son. The associated operations provisions should not apply: as Harman J said in *Bambridge* v *IRC* [1954] 1 WLR 1265 "Death avers Peter Pan is an awfully big adventure, but the Inland Revenue has not yet claimed that it is an associated operation".

The £2,000 exemption

GENERALLY

A donor may give away during his lifetime up to £2,000 each tax year without liability to capital transfer tax. If the exemption is unused in the year it can be carried forward to the next, but no further, as follows:

Tax year	*Exemption available*	*Gift made*	*Carry forward*
1978/79	£2,000	nil	£2,000
1979/80	£4,000	£1,900	£ 100
1980/81	£2,100	£2,000	nil

So any carry-forward must be used in the next tax year, or it will be lost.

The most tax efficient uses of this exemption are:

(*a*) creating and adding to a pure discretionary settlement (see p 51) or to an accumulation and maintenance settlement;
(*b*) paying out of capital the premium on a policy on the donor's life, which the donor has assigned to the donee. The normal expenditure out of income exemption should apply if payments are made out of income (see below). Life assurance relief for income tax should also be available;
(*c*) the exemption is sometimes used to pass on property using a sale and mortgage back arrangement (see below).

SALE AND MORTGAGE BACK ARRANGEMENTS

A parent who wishes to pass on to his child, eg a country cottage taking advantage of the £2,000 exemption (and the £250 exemption) would have practical difficulties of cost and valuation if he were to convey to the child each year £2,250 worth of the property and in any event the associated operations provisions would almost certainly apply so that when the final transfer is made, the parent will be treated as having given away the whole of the property at that time and at its value then.

Another way is for the parent to sell the property to the child, leaving the purchase price outstanding on mortgage. Each year the parent would write off the loan at a rate of £2,250. The Inland Revenue view on this was stated in a letter published in the *Law Society's Gazette* on 1 March 1978, in which they said:

> "the sale of the asset and the writing off of the loans are associated with each other as a single arrangement and, *prima facie*, we would consider FA 1975, s 44 (associated operations) relevant, whether or not interest was payable on the loan. If FA 1975, s 44 does apply it may well follow that under FA 1975, s 44(3) we would have to look at the value of the asset at the date of the release of the last part of the debt."

On the other hand, it could be that if, in these circumstances, the parent gave the child £2,250 each year and the child happened to use this to repay the loan, the Inland Revenue would not seek to apply the associated operations provisions. In the same letter in the *Law*

Society's Gazette, the Inland Revenue took the example of a gift of shares on terms that the son would pay the capital transfer tax by instalments, the father subsequently making further gifts of cash to the son, and said:

> "In this case we agree that FA 1975, s 44 does not apply; the mere fact that the father made later gifts within the annual exemption to enable the son to pay the tax would not therefore require the value transferred by the original gift to be reviewed.".

The annual £250 exemption

The amount of this exemption was increased from £100 to £250 by the FA 1980, s 86 for the tax year 1980/81 onwards. It only applies to outright lifetime gifts and enables the taxpayer to make each tax year any number of gifts of £250 each, to separate persons.

There is an esoteric argument which concludes that the £250 exemption and £2,000 exemption are mutually exclusive, but they are treated by the Inland Revenue as being additional to each other.

Best use of this exemption can be made:

(*a*) in making small gifts to children over and above the £2,000 exemption;

(*b*) on paying out of capital premiums on insurance policies (see £2,000 exemption also, above).

The normal expenditure out of income exemption

A gift is exempt if it is shown:

(*a*) that it was part of the normal expenditure of the transferor; and

(*b*) that (taking one year with another) it was made out of his income; and

(*c*) that, after allowing for all transfers of value forming part of his normal expenditure, the transferor was left with sufficient income to maintain his usual standard of living.

"Normal" is taken by the Inland Revenue as meaning habitual and it would appear that some element of repetition may be necessary, although no legally binding obligation to continue to make the payments need exist.

The most important uses of the exemption are:
(*a*) in paying out of income, premiums on gifted insurance policies;
(*b*) exempting interest free loans (see below);
(*c*) exempting maintenance payments to a former spouse and children which may not be covered by the exemption for dispositions for the maintenance of the family;
(*d*) exempting payments made under deeds of covenant.
The exemption only applies to lifetime transfers.

Dispositions for the maintenance of the family

This exemption is designed to exempt everyday maintenance of children, eg the payment of school fees for children and to apply to financial arrangements made on marriage breakdown. By FA 1975, s 46, a disposition is not a transfer of value if it is made by one party to a marriage in favour of the other party or of a child of either party and is for the maintenance of the other party or for the maintenance, education or training of the child for a period ending not later than the year in which the child attains the age of 18, or if later, ceases to undergo full-time education or training. Spouses are normally covered by the spouse exemption, but it is provided that "marriage" includes a former marriage "in relation to a disposition made on the occasion of the dissolution or annulment of a marriage, and in relation to a disposition varying a disposition so made" (FA 1975, s 46(6)), so maintenance on marriage breakdown is intended to be covered after the spouse exemption ceases.

The exemption undoubtedly covers maintenance for children whether before or after marriage breakdown, and is presumably designed to supplement the normal expenditure exemption (see above) in cases where maintenance is paid out of capital, or where the parent can ill afford the maintenance. It does not appear to cover the transfer of property to a child unless perhaps that property is a house in which it is intended that the child should live. If this happened, unless the house had to be given back when the child reached the age of 18, part of the gift would be outside the scope of the exemption and thus chargeable (FA 1975, s 46(5)).

The exemption is particularly appropriate to cover the

everyday maintenance of children and this includes the creation of an accumulation and maintenance settlement set up to pay a child's school fees, provided the provision could not continue past the child's eighteenth birthday or, if later, the time when he ceased full-time education or training.

The exemption only applies to lifetime transfers.

2.08 Lending property

In many cases, a parent may prefer to lend property to a child rather than give it to him outright or put it into a settlement for his benefit. The capital transfer tax rules for this are contained in FA 1976, ss 115–117 and apply when an individual allows another person the use of money or property for less than full consideration. The rules do not apply where the money or property is lent for a specified term, eg a 99 year lease at a peppercorn rent, since in this case it is possible to calculate the individual's loss on normal principles using actuarial calculations and capital transfer tax is charged when the property is first lent.

Where FA 1976, s 115 applies, the lender is treated as making each year a disposition of the difference between the cost to him of allowing the use and any consideration paid. The cost is deemed to be:

Money or land

In the case of money or land, the consideration which the lender might reasonably expect on a similar transaction at arm's length, less income tax thereon, is at the lender's top rate. There are no guidelines laid down by FA 1976 to determine what consideration is obtainable in these circumstances.

Other property

In the case of other property, eg chattels, the cost is the annual value of the use of the property plus expenditure thereon.

If a transaction is caught by FA 1976, s 115, the normal expenditure exemption is modified and is:

(*a*) that the transfer is a normal one on the part of the transferor; and

(*b*) that, after allowing for all the transfers of value forming part of his normal expenditure, the transferor was left with sufficient income to maintain his usual standard of living.

It is clear that a taxpayer liable to high income tax rates can lend his children his money or land with very little, if any, capital transfer tax liability. The normal expenditure exemption should be applicable to many transactions and the loan of property to a child could be a sensible alternative to an outright gift or settlement where the parent wants to retain control over the gifted property.

Example

A lends his adult child £10,000 repayable on demand. A could have received 15 per cent bank deposit interest on this amount and his top rate of income tax is 75 per cent.

A will be treated as making a disposition each year of 25 per cent of £1,500 = £375, while the loan is outstanding. This should be covered by exemptions. Even a loan of £100,000 produces an annual disposition of only £3,750.

2.09 Insurance policies

Insurance policies are very useful for the parent who wishes to confer a substantial tax free benefit on his child. There are two ways in which this can be done:

(*a*) the parent takes out a policy on his own life and assigns it to the child but continues to pay the premiums. When the policy moneys become payable to the child no capital transfer tax or capital gains tax is payable. Each payment of a premium should be within one of the annual exemptions, eg the normal expenditure out of income exemption, and should therefore attract no capital transfer tax. The parent should also be able to claim life assurance relief for income tax. If the parent pays the child the cash to enable the child to pay the premiums instead, the same capital transfer tax consequences arise but neither parent nor child will be able to claim life assurance relief;

(*b*) the child takes out a policy on his own life and the parent pays the premiums. Again the annual capital transfer tax exemptions should apply to the premiums and no capital tax liability arises on maturity. No life assurance relief is given, though, unless the child himself pays the premiums (funded by the parent), and the Inland Revenue will only allow the relief if the child has attained the age of 12 (see Inland Revenue Statement of Practice SP 11/79 dated 1 November 1979).

Chapter 3

CAPITAL SETTLEMENTS

3.01 Why make a settlement?

It needs a good reason to put capital into a settlement or Will trust and tie it up for a number of years instead of making an outright gift to the donee, and there are many. The most important reasons are:

(*a*) the donee may be too immature to handle the amounts involved. This clearly applies to minors and often applies to those of less tender years. A settlement provides the answer to the fear that the donee will turn out to be improvident or a wastrel;

(*b*) the donor may wish to retain some personal control over the property he is giving away, so he may well settle the property and appoint himself a trustee;

(*c*) tax is a very important reason. Income tax, capital gains tax and capital transfer tax can all be saved by the use of a settlement. For example, the maximum rate of income tax on accumulated income is 45 per cent, the maximum rate for an individual is 75 per cent. Again, if at some time in the future a child is to be given an asset which is likely in the meantime to appreciate in value rapidly, less capital transfer tax and capital gains tax will be incurred if the gift is made into a settlement now rather than as an outright gift later;

(*d*) settlements are also useful to provide funds for

school fees (see Chapter 5) although because of ICTA 1970, s 437, parents of minor children should not usually create a settlement solely for this purpose – a less onerous financial and fiscal result can be achieved by meeting the school fees out of current expenditure on an *ad hoc* basis;

(*e*) marriage breakdown may provide an occasion for the use of a settlement on children and the court may decide to exercise its power under the Matrimonial Causes Act 1973, s 24 to order a settlement for the benefit of a child of the family.

Usually the most tax efficient form of settlement for children of up to 25 years of age is the capital transfer tax accumulation and maintenance settlement, a form of discretionary settlement, but in certain circumstances a pure discretionary settlement may have advantages. For children who have reached the age of 25, the appropriate form of settlement will be one where they have the right to income, ie an interest in possession or fixed interest settlement. Before dealing with the options available, however, it is necessary to cover the minefield of income tax anti-avoidance provisions which are common to all types of settlement.

3.02 Income tax on the settlor: the anti-avoidance provisions

The scope

This Chapter is concerned with capital settlements, ie those where the settlor transfers part of his capital to trustees to hold on the trusts of a settlement, as opposed to income settlements which are usually covenants to pay income. The anti-avoidance provisions in ICTA 1970, ss 434–459 are common to both types of settlement but their application to income settlements is dealt with in Chapter 4.

The following rules apply to "settlements" which are defined by ICTA 1970, s 454(3) as including "any disposition, trust, covenant, agreement or arrangement". In the case of children's settlements, the expression also includes "transfer of assets" (ICTA 1970, s 444(2)) and for the 6 year rule, the provisions apply to "dispositions" which are defined to include "any trust, covenant, agreement or arrangement".

The apparently wide scope of these expressions has been cut down by the courts and it was confirmed by the House of Lords in *IRC* v *Plummer* [1979] STC 793 that the expression "settlement" only applies to transactions which include an element of bounty and not to all transactions which are not *bona fide* transactions. Most settlements will contain an element of bounty, but settlements made on marriage breakdown either by negotiation or under a court order may well not contain an element of bounty so that in such cases, any attempt by the Inland Revenue to impose the anti-avoidance provisions should be resisted.

The Inland Revenue have long taken the view that a court order to make payments direct to a person is not a settlement within these provisions.

Now that FA 1980, ss 55 and 56 has made it possible to make a 3 year plus covenant in favour of charity fully effective for income tax, the tide against settlements, which has been flooding in for the last 50 years, may at last be turning. In the meantime, however, the settlor is faced with the following provisions, all of which deem the income of the settlement to be his either for all rates of income tax or for the excess liability (ie the excess of the higher rates over the basic rate plus the investment income surcharge) only. The provisions assume the settlor to be alive, so they do not apply to Will trusts.

The 6 year rule (ICTA 1970, s 434)

Income payable by virtue or in consequence of a disposition (see above) for a period which cannot exceed 6 years, remains that of the settlor for all income tax purposes. This is primarily concerned with covenants (see p 56) but appears to include interest free loans for example. Payments made for valuable and sufficient consideration are excluded.

Example

A father lends his adult son £10,000 interest free, repayable in three years time, to help him through college. The son invests the money in a Building

Society and uses the income to meet his daily needs. Since the loan is made under an agreement or arrangement which cannot exceed 6 years, it is open to the Inland Revenue to treat the income from the Building Society as that of the father and he will be taxed on it (no capital transfer tax should be payable by virtue of FA 1975 s 46, see p 26).

Solution

The loan should be made repayable on demand, so that it could at the date of the disposition, exceed 6 years. The fact that the father calls in the loan after 3 years, is irrelevant. ICTA 1970, s 457 would apply, however (see below).

ICTA 1970, s 435 enables the settlor to recover from the beneficiary or trustees the tax which he has to pay as a result of ICTA 1970, s 434.

Children settlements (ICTA 1970, ss 437 and 438)

Income from a settlement payable to or for the benefit of the infant unmarried child of the settlor, is treated as the settlor's for all income tax purposes. This includes income which may become payable or applicable to or for the benefit of such a child but there is an exception for income accumulated under an irrevocable settlement of capital. A settlement will be treated as irrevocable broadly so long as neither the settlor nor his spouse can benefit under it.

Example 1

A creates an accumulation and maintenance settlement for his children. The settlement is irrevocable. Accumulated income will be taxed at 45 per cent and will not be treated as that of A. However, income distributed for the benefit of A's minor children (eg under the Trustee Act 1925, s 31) will be treated as A's. Income accumulated in previous years will also be treated as A's income when distributed to his minor children, as will distributions of capital, if there is undistributed income or accumulated income in the settlement.

Example 2

A makes a settlement on his son for life with remainder to his grandchildren. The son releases his life interest so that his minor children become entitled. Although the main settlement is not a parent settlement, the release is a disposition within ICTA 1970, s 437 and the income payable to the minor grandchildren will be treated as that of the son for income tax purposes (see *IRC* v *Buchanan* [1958] Ch 289 and *D'Abreu* v *IRC* [1978] STC 538).

As for ICTA 1970, s 434, there are provisions enabling the settlor to recover from the trustees or beneficiaries, the extra tax he has to pay under ICTA 1970, s 437.

Revocable settlements (ICTA 1970, s 446)

ICTA 1970, s 446 deems the income of a settlement to

be that of the settlor for all income tax purposes to the extent that there is an immediate or future power to revoke the settlement or to diminish the settlement or payments to be made out of it, if as a result the settlor or his spouse would benefit. If the power cannot be exercised for the first 6 years of the life of the settlement, the section does not apply so long as the power is not exercisable.

The power of revocation must be contained in the settlement itself.

Example

A settles property on trust for the benefit of such of his children as attain the age of 25 with power to revoke the settlement as to the potential share of any child who fails to reach 25. Since on normal trust principles a share if revoked would revert to the settlor and since the power extends to the whole settlement, all the settlement income is caught by ICTA 1970, s 446.

As for ICTA 1970, ss 434 and 437, the settlor may recover from the trustees or beneficiaries the extra tax he has to pay as a result of this section.

Discretionary power for the benefit of the settlor or his spouse (ICTA 1970, s 448)

By ICTA 1970, s 448, if the settlor or his spouse is an object of a discretionary power contained in the settlement, the income is treated as that of the settlor for all income tax purposes. If the power cannot be exercised for the first 6 years of the life of the settlement, the section does not apply so long as the power is not exercisable. Nor does the section apply if the power is only exercisable on the happening of certain specified events, eg the death under 25 of a person who would be entitled on reaching that age.

Example

A settles property on trust for the benefit of such of his children as shall attain the age of 25, giving the trustees power to apply income or capital among a class which includes the settlor or his spouse. The income of the settlement is caught by ICTA 1970, s 448. If it were accumulated, ICTA 1970, s 447 (see below) would also apply.

As for previous sections, the settlor may recover the extra tax he has to pay as a result of the section.

Accumulated income

Income accumulated under a settlement will be treated as that of the settlor for all income tax purposes in the following circumstances:

SETTLOR RETAINS AN INTEREST (ICTA 1970, S 447)

ICTA 1970, s 447 applies if under the terms of the settlement, income or capital of the settlement may, in whatever circumstances, be applicable to or for the benefit of the settlor or his spouse, except on the happening of certain specified events, eg the death under 25 of a person who would be entitled on reaching that age.

Example 1

A settles property on his grandson for life with remainder to the grandson's issue. The grandson is a minor and income is accumulated under the Trustee Act 1925, s 31. Since the grandson may have no issue, the settled property could revert to the settlor. All accumulated income will therefore be treated as that of the settlor.

It is usual to make a specific provision in a settlement deed that the settlor and his spouse are excluded from all benefit. It will therefore be necessary to make a gift of the settled property to an ultimate beneficiary in case all other interests fail.

Example 2

A settles property for the benefit of such of his children who attain the age of 25. If all his children fail to reach that age, the settled property will revert to A, but ICTA 1970, s 447 does not apply because interest arises only on one of the except specified events.

As for previous sections, the settlor may recover the extra tax he has to pay.

SUMS PAID BY THE SETTLOR (ICTA 1970, S 450)

ICTA 1970, s 450 catches accumulated income to the extent that the settlor pays into the settlement sums which would otherwise be deductible in computing his total income, eg covenanted sums and interest payments.

In this case there is no provision enabling the settlor to recover from the trustees or beneficiaries the extra tax he has to pay.

SUMS PAID TO THE SETTLOR (ICTA 1970, S 451)

This is an important section if for no other reason than that it is insufficiently well known. It catches capital sums paid directly or indirectly by the trustees of a settlement to the settlor or his spouse, to the extent that income remains undistributed. To calculate the settlor's income tax liability, the sum must be grossed up at the basic rate and additional rate of income tax, but there is no provision for giving a credit for the 45 per cent. If the accumulated income is insufficient in one year, the capital sum paid is carried forward without time limit.

The section is very wide: capital sums include loans and repayments of loans and any sum paid to the settlor by a company is deemed to have been paid by the trustees of the settlement if the company is close and the trustees or beneficiaries are participators.

Example

A sets up a company in which shares are held as to 49 per cent by A and his wife and as to 51 per cent by an accumulation and maintenance trust for A's minor children. A lends the company £10,000 to start up the business and this is repaid to him over the next 5 years. These repayments are capital sums within ICTA 1970, s 451. If, from then on, settlement income is accumulated, it will be treated as the settlors up to £10,000 grossed-up. While the children are still minors, settlement income distributed will also be treated as the settlor's. The settlor is, therefore, caught between the devil and the deep blue sea, but ICTA 1970, s 437 is somewhat less onerous than ICTA 1970, s 451, particularly as the extra tax payable under ICTA 1970, s 437 can be recovered by the settlor. ICTA 1970, s 451 contains no such provision.

The capital sums must be paid to the settlor himself or to his spouse. Any sum paid direct to a creditor of the settlor is not deemed to be paid to the settlor himself (*Potts Executors* v *IRC* [1951] AC 443). Thus if the trustees pay to the Inland Revenue direct the capital transfer tax payable on creation of the settlement, ICTA 1970, s 451 does not apply (see p 53). The Revenue are currently considering substantial amendments to s 451.

Excess liability on the settlor (ICTA 1970, s 457)

By ICTA 1970, s 457, income from a settlement will be treated as that of the settlor for the purposes of calculating his liability to the excess of the higher rates of income tax and to the additional rate over the basic rate (the sums caught being treated as the settlor's investment income, regardless of whether they originated from earned or investment income (*Ang* v *Parrish* [1980] STC 341), unless the income is either:

(*a*) income from property of which the settlor has absolutely divested himself except on the happening of certain specified events, eg the death under 25 of a person who would be entitled on reaching that age; or

(*b*) income from a settlement on a divorced or separated spouse; or
(*c*) payments made under a partnership agreement to or for the benefit of a former partner, his widow, or dependants, and made for full consideration; or
(*d*) payments for the acquisition of a partnership interest made for full consideration;
(*e*) covenanted payments not exceeding £3,000 pa made to a charity.

If the right to payments made under (*c*) and (*d*) devolves on the death of a partner to a person other than a widow or dependant of that partner, ICTA 1970, s 457 only catches such of the payments as are made later than ten years after the partner ceased to be a member of the partnership.

The section often overlaps with the other anti-avoidance provisions; if it does, the other anti-avoidance provisions apply and s 457 is disregarded.

Example
A settles property on trust for B if he attains the age of 30. The property will revert to A if B fails to attain that age. While B is a minor, income may be accumulated under Trustee Act 1925, s 31. If it is, ICTA 1970, s 447 will apply. ICTA 1970, s 457 applies to distributed income, since the settlor has not absolutely divested himself of the settled capital. If ICTA 1970, s 457 does apply, A suffers the excess liability, B will only be liable to income tax at the basic rate.

Professional charging provisions

A settlement will usually contain a provision enabling professional (and sometimes lay) trustees to make a reasonable charge for the work which they do. If the settlor and his spouse are not excluded from this provision and if, as would usually be the case, they can be appointed trustees, it is open to the Inland Revenue to argue that the settlement income is caught by ICTA 1970, ss 446, 447 or, perhaps, 448. Whether such an argument would succeed remains to be seen, but clearly it is prudent to exclude the settlor and his spouse from benefit under charging clauses.

3.03 Accumulation and maintenance settlements

The most flexible form of children's settlement would be one which gave the trustees a discretion over who should benefit from income or capital, for as long as possible. Since FA 1975, such a trust would be one without an interest in possession and would suffer from the adverse capital transfer tax consequences of discretionary settlements (see p 49). However, it is still possible to create a fiscally attractive discretionary settlement in favour of children, provided it falls within the definition of an accumulation and maintenance settlement under FA 1975, Sched 5, para 15.

Definition

An accumulation and maintenance settlement is a settlement where:

(*a*) one or more persons ("beneficiaries") will, on or before attaining a specified age not exceeding 25, become entitled to, or to an interest in possession in, the settled property or part of it; and

(*b*) no interest in possession subsists in the settled property or part and the income from it is to be accumulated so far as not applied for the maintenance, education or benefit of a beneficiary; and

(*c*) either:

(i) not more than 25 years have elapsed since the day on which the settlement was made or if it was later, since the time (or latest time) when the conditions stated in paragraphs (*a*) and (*b*) above became satisfied with respect to the property or part; or

(ii) all the persons who are or have been beneficiaries are or were either grandchildren of a common grandparent or children, widows or widowers of such grandchildren who were themselves beneficiaries but died before the time when had they survived they would have become entitled as mentioned in paragraph (*a*) above.

Operation of the Trustee Act 1925, s 31

THE LAW

Unless it is excluded by the settlement, the Trustee Act 1925, s 31 will always apply and it provides that when property is held on trust for a person, for whatever interest, then subject to prior interests:

(*a*) until that person attains the age of 18 (21 if the

settlement was created before 1 January 1970), the trustees may apply the income for his maintenance, education or benefit, but to the extent that they do not, they must accumulate the income;

(*b*) at age 18 (or 21), the income must be paid over to the beneficiary, even if his interest is contingent only;

(*c*) accumulations accrue to capital at 18 (or 21), but if the beneficiary had a vested right to income during his minority (ie no contingency such as attainment of full age had to be satisfied), he must be paid over the accumulations at age 18. An example of a vested interest in income is a settlement on A for life even though A is a minor (*Stanley* v *IRC* [1944] 1 KB 225).

It will be seen that up to age 18 the trusts in (*a*) are the same as those in FA 1975, Sched 5, para 15, but that at 18, the beneficiary acquires a right to the income ie an interest in possession and the accumulation and maintenance settlement ceases then. But does this acquisition of an interest in possession take place at a "specified age", as required by para 15? The Inland Revenue accept that it does; by Extra Statutory Concession F8, the requirement that a beneficiary should become entitled at a specified age is regarded as being satisfied if it is clear that the beneficiary will in fact become entitled by the age of 25.

OUSTING THE TRUSTEE ACT 1925, S 31 AND THE ALTERNATIVE ACCUMULATION PERIODS

The Trustee Act 1925, s 31 applies only if there is no contrary intention shown in the settlement. Generally an express direction to accumulate income past the age of majority will oust the Trustee Act 1925, s 31 and it is advisable also to include in the settlement an express power to apply income for the maintenance education or benefit of the beneficiary. The question is to what extent it is permissible to accumulate income other than under the statutory power under the Trustee Act 1925, s 31. The answer is provided by the Law of Property Act 1925, s 164 and the Perpetuities and Accumulations Act 1964 and the permitted accumulation periods include:

(*a*) the life of the settlor;

(*b*) 21 years from the date of the settlement;

(*c*) the minority or respective minorities of beneficiaries who would be entitled to the income if of full age.

Careful drafting is needed to substitute one of these

periods for the Trustee Act 1925, s 31, and it is crucial to remember the requirement that a beneficiary *will* on or before attaining a specified age not exceeding 25, become entitled. Thus by using the 21 year period, it is possible to continue to the accumulation and maintenance trusts till a beneficiary reaches 25, but only if he is already at least 4 years old. However the settlement must ensure that the power to accumulate ceases as to the share of each beneficiary when he or she reaches 25. If the power to accumulate continues past that age, the settlement will at no time be an accumulation and maintenance settlement.

The capital transfer tax consequences (FA 1975, Sched 5, para 15(2) and (3))

The capital transfer tax reliefs for accumulation and maintenance settlements are considerable. They are:

(*a*) on creation of the settlement. This gives rise to the normal capital transfer tax consequences of a gift. The lifetime exemptions (or if the settlement is a Will trust, those exemptions applicable to death) may be used, although the £250 exemption does not apply to gifts into settlement;

(*b*) until the beneficiary reaches the specified age, no capital transfer tax is payable on distributions to him, nor is the periodic charge to capital transfer tax, payable;

(*c*) when the beneficiary becomes entitled to the trust property or to an interest in possession, no capital transfer tax is charged;

(*d*) if a settlement is converted into an accumulation and maintenance settlement, capital transfer tax is payable. If the settlement had no interest in possession, the conversion is treated as a capital distribution. If the settlement had an interest in possession, capital transfer tax is charged as if the owner of that interest had made a gift of the trust property.

The capital gains tax consequences (CGTA 1979, ss 53–56)

(*a*) on creation of the settlement, capital gains tax will be payable as if the settlor had disposed of the settled property at market value. The hold-over relief for gifts in FA 1980 does not apply to gifts into settlement although the relief for gifts of business assets under CGTA 1979, s 126 can apply.

(*b*) when a beneficiary becomes absolutely entitled to capital, either on reaching the specified age, or before, as a result of an appointment out or advancement of capital, capital gains tax is payable. The trustees are treated as disposing of the property concerned at market value, and immediately reacquiring it;
(*c*) when a beneficiary becomes entitled to an interest in possession only, no capital gains tax is payable;
(*d*) if a settlement is converted into an accumulation and maintenance settlement, capital gains tax will be payable if, before conversion a beneficiary had a life interest. If the settlement was discretionary, capital gains tax will only be payable if the old settlement is wholly superseded. If some provisions of the old settlement still subsist, no capital gains tax should be payable (*Hoare* v *Gardner, Hart* v *Briscoe* [1978] STC 89). A rough and ready rule is that if a special power of appointment (ie exercisable amongst a limited or designated class only) is used, no capital gains tax is payable. If a power of advancement (eg under Trustee Act 1925, s 32) or general power of appointment is used, capital gains tax will be levied (see Inland Revenue Statement of Practice SP7/78).

The income tax consequences

Subject to the anti-avoidance rules in 3.02, accumulated income is taxed at the basic and additional rates of tax (30 per cent + 15 per cent = 45 per cent for 1980/81). Income distributed to or for the benefit of a beneficiary is grossed-up and included in his total income with a recoverable credit for the basic and additional rates of tax deducted. If the beneficiary has a vested interest in income (eg to A for life; A has a vested interest in income) even though it is accumulated, he will be liable to income tax on the income as it arises (*Stanley* v *IRC* [1944] 1 KB 225) and the additional rate of tax will not be levied on the trustees.

Planning points

CLOSING THE CLASS OF BENEFICIARIES

The potential beneficiaries of an accumulation and maintenance settlement should not include those who can be born after the first beneficiary has reached the specified age, which if the Trustee Act 1925, s 31 applies, will be 18. If after this time a beneficiary is born, it will reduce the interest in possession of the first beneficiary and give rise to a capital transfer tax and capital gains tax charge. This can be avoided by closing the class of beneficiaries when the first reaches the specified age, eg those of the children of A who attain the age of 25 and who are born before the first child of A attains an interest in possession in the Trust Fund.

CHILD BORROWING

For an accumulation and maintenance settlement to exist, there must at some time have been a living beneficiary. If there is none, a capital transfer tax charge arises when the first is born and the periodic charge can arise in the meanwhile. These charges can be avoided by "borrowing" a living child and making him or her a beneficiary but:

(*a*) to ensure the settlement can continue as an accumulation and maintenance settlement for longer than 25 years, the borrowed child should be the first cousin of the unborn beneficiaries;

(*b*) unless it is desired to give the borrowed child a substantial benefit, there must be a power for the trustees to vary the shares of each beneficiary in the settlement (see below);

(*c*) if no other beneficiary is born (or adopted) before the borrowed child attains an interest in possession, the purpose of borrowing him will be defeated – either he takes the lot, or if he loses the whole or part of his interest when another beneficiary is born subsequently, he will incur a substantial capital transfer tax and capital gains tax charge.

SHARE VARIATIONS

It is possible to include in an accumulation and maintenance settlement a power for the trustees to increase or decrease the presumptive share of any beneficiary. However, this power must be drafted with caution. It must always be possible to say that a beneficiary *will* become entitled on attaining the specified age. Thus if the power to vary shares enables the trustees to increase the share of a beneficiary who has already attained the specified age, it cannot be said that the other beneficiaries *will* themselves become entitled – the trustees could give their shares, or part, to the first, and the settlement will not be an accumulation and maintenance settlement.

If the power enables the trustees to reduce the share of a beneficiary who has reached the specified age, the exercise of the power would give rise to a capital transfer tax charge in respect of the loss of his interest in possession.

Clearly, therefore, the power to vary shares should only be exercisable in respect of the shares of those under the specified age, and in favour of the same. It can then always be said that one or more of those beneficiaries will become entitled on reaching the specified age.

DEFERRING THE VESTING OF CAPITAL

The accumulation and maintenance provisions envisage a beneficiary becoming entitled either to income or to capital on reaching the specified age. Is it possible to give the primary beneficiaries life interests only and on their death create an accumulation and maintenance settlement for their issue? An example would be a gift to the children of A who attain the age of 18 for life with remainder to their issue at 21. The advantage is that the primary beneficiaries can never demand capital as of right so it can be kept back from them, although the trustees can be, and usually are given specific power to pay it over to them if they think fit. The problem lies in the definition (see p 39) which permits an accumulation and maintenance settlement to continue for 25 years only unless all the beneficiaries are brothers, sisters and first cousins, with a substitutional provision for their children or widows or widowers but only if the principal beneficiaries fail to attain the specified age.

The answer is that it is possible to defer the vesting of capital in this way. When the accumulation and maintenance settlement is created, the class of beneficiaries is restricted to brothers, sisters and first cousins with the appropriate substitutional provision. This satisfies the definition. After each attains a life interest, the settlement ceases to be an accumulation and maintenance settlement as regards that share. When the principal beneficiaries die, the property is held on trust for their issue and as to each share the settlement will again become an accumulation and maintenance settlement and this may last up to twenty-five years, since the temporal restriction applies from the *latest* time that the relevant conditions are satisfied. If vesting of capital is to be deferred, the rule against perpetuities must always be borne in mind when drafting the relevant provisions.

VESTING AT AGE 17: SAVING CAPITAL GAINS TAX

If property is settled on A if he attains the age of 17, until he reaches that age, the property remains settled for both capital gains tax (CGTA 1979, s 46(1)) and capital transfer tax (FA 1975, Sched 5, para 1(2)(*a*)). When A attains the age of 17, the property ceases to be settled property for capital gains tax because it is now held on trust for a person who would be absolutely entitled but for being an infant. However, no charge to capital gains tax arises under CGTA 1979, s 54 because A is not in fact absolutely entitled as he is not yet of age. The rider to the s 46 definition of settlement "but for being an infant" does not apply to CGTA 1979, s 54. Since for capital gains tax the property ceases to be settled property when A reaches 17, no further charge can arise when he reaches 18 and capital gains tax is avoided.

For capital transfer tax, the trust will be an accumulation and maintenance settlement until A reaches 18, when Trustee Act 1925, s 31 will cease to apply. No capital transfer tax will be levied then nor when A attains the age of 17.

CONVERTING EXISTING SETTLEMENTS: TRUSTEE ACT 1925, S 32

Discretionary settlements suffer substantial capital transfer tax disadvantages, eg the periodic charge (see p 49). Converting such a settlement into one less harshly treated, eg an accumulation and maintenance settlement, gives rise to a capital transfer tax charge and possibly a capital gains tax charge. However, by FA 1975, Sched 5, para 14, the capital transfer tax charge on discretionary settlements created before 27 March 1974 is levied at 20 per cent of the rate which would normally be charged, provided the capital distribution is made before 1 April 1982.

In a wide discretionary settlement there will almost certainly be a wide special power of appointment enabling the trustees to appoint new trusts over the capital of the settlement, so conversion into an accumulation and maintenance settlement should give rise to no difficulty. If, however, such a power does not exist, the trustees might consider using their power of advancement under the Trustee Act 1925, s 32. This enables trustees to pay or apply up to one-half of the presumptive share of a beneficiary in the capital of a settlement, for his advancement or benefit. It was held by the House of Lords in *Pilkington* v *IRC* [1964] AC 612 that this power could be exercised to advance property into a new settlement for the benefit of the beneficiary. The new settlement could be an accumulation and maintenance settlement; the disadvantage is that the other half of the presumptive share will be left in the original settlement. Capital gains tax would also be payable when the advancement is made (see *Hart* v *Briscoe*, p 42). The Trustee Act 1925, s 32 cannot be used in favour of a beneficiary with an income interest only.

Uses for accumulation and maintenance settlements

If a United Kingdom resident children's settlement is to be created, the vehicle should almost always be an accumulation and maintenance settlement because of the substantial capital transfer tax advantages. In the light of the tax provisions already discussed, an accumulation and maintenance settlement would be particularly appropriate in the following circumstances:

(*a*) where the settlor has an asset which is likely to appreciate rapidly in value. If he has young children, it would be better to settle the property now, crystallising the capital tax liability rather than wait till later when a gift of the asset would give rise to considerable capital transfer tax. The disadvantage is that capital gains tax is payable on the gift of the property into the settlement whereas as the law now stands, on an outright gift of the property at some future time, it could be postponed provided both donor and donee agree;

(*b*) if an existing discretionary settlement, created before 27 March 1974 has to be converted, it is always advantageous to convert it into an accumulation and maintenance settlement;

(*c*) an accumulation and maintenance settlement can be suitable as an investment vehicle to be used to pay children's school fees. A parent should not create such a settlement because of the adverse income tax consequences;

(*d*) an accumulation and maintenance settlement is a suitable vehicle to which to grant an option over shares (see p 102);

(*e*) Will Trusts can take the form of an accumulation and maintenance settlement.

3.04 Fixed interest settlements

If a beneficiary is entitled to the income of a settlement and the trustees have no power to accumulate it (see *Pearson* v *IRC* [1980] STC 318), he has for capital transfer tax an interest in possession and by FA 1975, Sched 5, para 3 is treated as owning the settled property. For capital gains tax he will probably have a life interest. The beneficiary entitled to the remainder (in the 1975 Act called a reversion) is treated for capital transfer tax as owning nothing. The following examples show the tax consequences and potential of such settlements:

To A for life remainder to B. The trust property is worth £100

A DIES

Capital transfer tax will be levied on the £100 as part of A's estate, at his estate rate FA 1975, ss 22(1) and 23.

For capital gains tax, as B becomes absolutely entitled there will be a notional disposal and reacquisition of the settled property at market value (CGTA 1979, s 54) but by CGTA 1979, s 56, no capital gains tax is payable.

If B were the settlor, on A's death no capital transfer tax would be payable because the settled property reverts to the settlor, FA 1975, s 22(2), so long as B had not acquired his interest for money or money's worth. On the other hand, for capital gains tax, when settled property reverts to the settlor, the disposal and reacquisition under CGTA 1979, s 54 above is treated as taking place at such a consideration as shall secure that neither gain nor loss arises to the trustees (CGTA 1979, s 56(1)(*b*)).

A ASSIGNS HIS LIFE INTEREST

For capital transfer tax, A is treated as giving away the settled property and capital transfer tax is leviable at his rates, the amount of the gift being reduced by any consideration received by A. The non-gratuitous exemption under FA 1975, s 20(4) does not apply. For capital gains tax, the disposal of a settlement interest is exempt if no consideration has been given for it (CGTA 1979, s 58).

B DIES OR ASSIGNS HIS LIFE INTEREST BEFORE DEATH OF A

If B were to die or assign his life interest before the death of A, no capital transfer tax nor capital gains tax would be payable as long as B had not acquired his interest for money or money's worth.

A IS SPOUSE OF SETTLOR: ESTATE DUTY PAYABLE ON DEATH OF SETTLOR

If A was the spouse of the settlor and when the settlor died estate duty was payable on his death, no capital transfer tax would be payable on the lifetime termination of A's interest (FA 1975, Sched 5, para 4(7)) nor on A's death (FA 1975, s 22(4)).

To A if he attains the age of 50

A IS UNDER 18

The Trustee Act 1925, s 31 applies, the trustees have power to apply the income for the maintenance, education or benefit of A and must otherwise accumulate it. The settlement is an accumulation and maintenance settlement.

A ATTAINS 18

The Trustee Act 1925, s 31 requires the income to be paid over to him, so he acquires an interest in possession. No capital transfer tax or capital gains tax is payable then.

A ATTAINS 50: THE TRUST CAPITAL IS PAID OVER TO A

No capital transfer tax is payable, but since A has become absolutely entitled, capital gains tax is payable under CGTA 1979, s 54.

Uses for fixed interest settlements

TO POSTPONE THE VESTING OF TRUST CAPITAL ON TERMINATION OF A SETTLEMENT

A fixed interest settlement can be used to postpone the vesting of trust capital after an accumulation and maintenance settlement comes to an end. Many settlors consider that the age of 18 or 25 is too young for a child to inherit substantial sums and a fixed interest settlement prevents the beneficiary from getting his hands on the capital. See also p 44 where the principal beneficiaries attained a life interest only and could never demand capital. The trustees will usually be given power to pay over capital to a beneficiary with a fixed interest, if they think fit.

DIVESTMENT OF RAPIDLY APPRECIATING CAPITAL BY SETTLOR

A fixed interest settlement is also useful where the settlor wishes to divest himself of capital which is rapidly appreciating in value and the beneficiary is too old for an accumulation and maintenance settlement, but insufficiently mature to cope with the capital.

3.05 Discretionary settlements

Where no-one is entitled to the income of a settlement, no interest in possession subsists and it can loosely be called a discretionary settlement, implying that the trustees have a discretion over how to distribute income. There may also be a discretion over capital but this will make no difference to the income entitlements, and a discretion over capital is often found in all types of settlement.

The charge to capital transfer tax

Unless a discretionary settlement is an accumulation and maintenance settlement or some other specifically privileged form of settlement, eg a charitable trust, the capital transfer tax consequences are disadvantageous. Tax is levied on capital distributions as on the value transferred by a chargeable transfer (FA 1975, Sched 5, para 6), eg on the following occasions:

(*a*) a payment out of the settlement which is neither the income of the recipient nor a payment of costs and expenses;

(*b*) when a person becomes entitled to an interest in possession;

(*c*) on the creation of an accumulation and maintenance settlement;

(*d*) at the relevant anniversary, ie the decennial periodic charge to capital transfer tax. The first charge cannot arise until 1 April 1982.

Grossing-up may be required if the capital transfer tax is not borne by the recipient of a payment out, or by the property concerned in the other cases. No grossing-up is required for the periodical charge.

Tax is always charged at the lifetime rates but the rate of tax depends on when the settlement was created. For those created after 26 March 1974, the following calculations are made to determine the rate of tax on capital distributions (FA 1975, Sched 5, para 7):

(*a*) calculate the market value of the settled property, ie its value immediately after creation of the settlement after all liabilities have been discharged;

(*b*) calculate the rate of tax the settlor would have paid if instead of the actual amount he transferred on creation of the settlement, he had transferred the initial value. No grossing-up is necessary; the up-to-date rates of tax are used;

(*c*) capital distributions are taxed at this rate up to a cumulative amount of the initial value (disregarding the periodic charge when cumulating);

(*d*) thereafter, the rate of tax on capital distributions is that which the settlor would have paid if he had added the distributions to the original settlement.

Pre 27 March 1974 settlements: what should be done

For settlements created before 27 March 1974, the rate of tax is determined by treating the settlement as an individual and cumulating distributions made out of it (FA 1975, Sched 5, para 8). Transitional relief is available for these settlements, tax being charged at 20 per cent of the rate otherwise chargeable if the capital distribution is made before 1 April 1982. Trustees will wish to take advantage of this relief, depending on the result of the review of capital taxes at present being conducted by the Government and there are three choices:

(*a*) distribute settlement property to a beneficiary outright;

(*b*) create an accumulation and maintenance settlement;

(*c*) create a fixed interest settlement.

Capital gains tax should only be payable in (*a*), and not in (*b*) and (*c*) (see p 41).

Is there scope for new discretionary settlements?

It is possible to create tax efficient discretionary settlements using the £2,000 exemption, as follows:

(*a*) create a wide discretionary trust including as beneficiaries the settlor and his spouse, if desired, and every person it is wished to benefit, giving the trustees power to add extra beneficiaries;

(*b*) the settlor and his spouse each contribute £2,000 cash every year;

(*c*) the £2,000 is invested by paying the premiums on a life policy on, say, the life of the settlor or his spouse;

(*d*) when the policy becomes payable, the trustees distribute the proceeds to whomsoever they wish.

No capital transfer tax should be payable provided the settlor and his spouse did not make chargeable transfers exceeding about £40,000 to £45,000 before paying each premium. The payment of each premium is treated as an addition to the settlement and the rate of tax calculated as for settlements created after 26 March 1974 above. In calculating the initial value, however, the £2,000 exemption must be ignored and this is why it is important that the settlors should not approach too near the £50,000 limit on chargeable transfers taxed at a nil rate. The rate of capital transfer tax on each premium will be nil and any profit attributable to each premium should also be within the nil rate band.

In this way a substantial benefit can be conferred without liability to capital transfer tax. Capital gains tax will not be payable and there will be no adverse income tax consequences since there will be no income in the settlement.

Discretionary settlements are also suitable for use as foreign settlements, which suffer no capital transfer tax nor capital gains tax provided the settlor is not domiciled in the United Kingdom and, for capital transfer tax, the settled property is outside the United Kingdom and, for capital gains tax, the trustees are neither resident nor ordinarily resident in the United Kingdom.

A discretionary settlement can be used in a Will (see p 118).

3.06 Can the settlor benefit from a children's settlement?

For tax reasons, the settlor may wish to settle certain assets but at the same time he may also wish to be able to revoke the settlement and have the property returned to him if the beneficiaries turn out to be undeserving. The tax consequences of this are:

Capital transfer tax

During the currency of the settlement there are no adverse consequences of the settlor's possible interest. If the settlor does revoke the settlement, however, no capital transfer tax will be payable whether the settlement is discretionary (FA 1975, Sched 5, para 6(*b*)) or is one with an interest in possession (FA 1975, Sched 5, para 4(5)) – the disadvantage is that the settlor's retained interest can prevent the existence of an accumulation and maintenance settlement unless his power to benefit or revoke is postponed until after the beneficiaries have acquired interests in possession.

Capital gains tax

No exemption applies if property reverts to the settlor during the lifetime of the beneficiaries of a settlement and capital gains tax is payable normally. If the settlor becomes absolutely entitled on the death of a beneficiary, the trustees are deemed to dispose of and immediately reacquire the settled property at such a consideration as gives rise to neither gain nor loss. Otherwise, capital gains tax is not payable on a death.

Income tax

If there is income in the settlement, ICTA 1970, ss 446, 447, 448, 451 and 457 could apply. However if the trust property is invested in non-income producing assets, the adverse income tax consequences disappear.

3.07 The settlor as trustee

In accumulation and maintenance settlements as in all other discretionary settlements, it can be of great practical advantage to the settlor to be a trustee. For example, the trust property may be shares in the family company over which he may wish to retain control (although he must exercise his vote for the benefit of the beneficiaries). If the settlor does become a trustee, he should bear in mind:

(*a*) that he should not be able to benefit from a charging clause (see p 38);

(*b*) that from a trust point of view, he must be seen to be acting wholly without regard to his own self interest and must on no account confuse his own assets with those of the trust.

3.08 Should the settlor burden the trustee with the capital tax liability on creation of the settlement?

If the trustees pay the capital transfer tax liability of the settlor when the settlement is created, no grossing-up is necessary, and capital transfer tax will be saved. If the trustees also meet the capital gains tax, the value transferred by the settlor's transfer is reduced.

There may be adverse income tax consequences, however. If the settlement specifically empowers the trustees to meet the settlor's capital tax liability, ICTA 1970, ss 447, 448 and 457 would apply to the trust income, but only until the liability is met. If the terms of the settlement are silent on the point, it is understood that the Revenue would not apply these provisions. The payment of the capital tax would also be a capital sum within ICTA 1970, s 451, so it is important that the trustees pay these taxes direct to the Inland Revenue and not to the settlor.

Chapter 4

DEEDS OF COVENANT

4.01 Generally

There is still considerable scope for tax saving with voluntary deeds of covenant in favour of children, although usually only at the basic rate of tax, so if the recipient is also taxed at the basic rate on the sum received, no overall tax advantage will be reaped.

Subject to the income tax anti-avoidance provisions dealt with below, if a covenant is to be effective at all, the payment must be an annual payment liable to income tax under Schedule D Case III, in the hands of the recipient. The case law (eg *IRC* v *Whitworth Park Coal Co Ltd* [1958] Ch 792) shows that to be an annual payment, a receipt must have four characteristics:

(*a*) it must be made under a legally binding obligation. In the case of voluntary payments, a deed is essential;

(*b*) it must be recurrent and capable of continuing for more than a year;

(*c*) it must be pure income profit in the hands of the recipient, eg not a reward for goods or services;

(*d*) it must be *ejusdem generis* with interest and annuities.

Payments under a properly drawn deed of covenant will satisfy these requirements and, subject to the income tax anti-avoidance provisions, will be payable under deduction of basic rate tax under ICTA 1970, ss 52 or 53 (see 4.03) and thus will be a charge on the payer's income, ie deductible in computing total income (see *Howe* v *IRC* [1919] 2 KB 336).

4.02 Income tax problems

Having established that a payment under a deed of covenant is otherwise an annual payment and thus *prima facie* liable in the recipient's hands to income tax under Schedule D Case III, the next step is to consider the relevant income tax anti-avoidance provisions in ICTA 1970. These have been dealt with in some detail in Chapter 3 and concern income tax settlements. A deed of covenant is within the income tax definition of settlement, and the arrangement is gratuitous. The effect of the anti-avoidance provisions on covenants is to restrict the tax relief given to the covenantor and the taxation of the recipient.

The 6 year rule (ICTA 1970, s 434)

The payments under the covenant must be capable of continuing for more than 6 years (in the case of covenants in favour of charities, FA 1980, s 55 reduced this period to 3 years). Seven year covenants are, therefore, the norm since payments thereunder should be capable of continuing for more than 6 years, but care must be taken when drafting the deed that the last payment is to be made more than 6 years after the first, or the payments will be caught by ICTA 1970, s 434 (see *IRC* v *St Luke's Hostel Trustees* 15 TC 682). The test is whether the payments can go on for more than 6 years, not whether they actually do go on for that period of time. Examples of periods satisfying ICTA 1970, s 434 are:

(*a*) until the beneficiary ceases to undergo full-time education or training – provided it is possible that such education or training could go on for more than 6 years;
(*b*) the life of the covenantor or recipient;

(*c*) until the taxable income of the recipient from other sources exceeds his personal reliefs.

The amount payable under the covenant must be a constant fixed sum or calculated with reference to a constant formula, for example:

(*a*) a specified sum, eg £2,000 pa;

(*b*) a stated fraction of the covenantor's income, eg 10 per cent of gross earnings per annum;

(*c*) an amount equal to the single person's relief each year.

If the covenant is caught by ICTA 1970, s 434, the payments thereunder must still be made, but for income tax purposes, they are treated as the income of the covenantor and not the income of any other person. This means that they are not a charge on the covenantor's income and since they are not the recipient's income under Schedule D Case III, they must be made without deducting basic rate income tax.

Infant unmarried children (ICTA 1970, s 437)

Covenants in favour of the covenantor's infant unmarried child are also totally ineffective for all tax purposes.

Excess liability on covenantors (ICTA 1970, s 457)

Covenants which do not fall foul of the other anti-avoidance provisions will, with certain limited exceptions (see p 37), fall foul of ICTA 1970, s 457 and thus the payments will remain the income of the covenantor (and not that of the recipient) when calculating liability to the excess of the higher rates over the basic rate of tax and to the additional rate of tax. This means that the covenant will only be effective for the basic rate of tax.

4.03 Taxation of covenantor and recipient: the tax collection procedures

If the covenant is totally ineffective for all tax purposes, eg under ICTA 1970, ss 434 and 437, the payments are ignored for income tax purposes; the covenantor is given no tax relief, the recipient is not taxed on the income and the payments are made gross. If the covenant falls foul of ICTA 1970, s 457 only or is fully effective for all income tax purposes, it is an annual payment in the recipient's hands liable to income tax under Schedule D Case III (at the basic rate only if ICTA 1970, s 457 applies), and thus the tax collection procedures under ICTA 1970, ss 52 or 53 will apply. Section 52 applies to the extent that the payment is made out of income brought into the charge of income tax (ie the payer has sufficient income to cover the payment) and the procedure is:

(*a*) the covenantor is assessed to basic rate tax only on the covenanted amount (ICTA 1970, ss 3 and 52(1)(*b*));

(*b*) when making the payment, the covenantor is entitled to deduct basic rate tax at the rate in force when the payment is due and make the payment net (ICTA 1970 s 52(1)(*c*), (*d*)), giving the recipient a tax deduction certificate in form R185;

(*c*) in the year in which it is due the recipient is assessed to income tax on the gross payment at all rates (at the basic rate only if ICTA 1970, s 457 applies), with a credit for the basic rate already deducted (ICTA 1970, s 52(1)(*e*)). To the extent that his liability to income tax is less than the credit, the recipient may recover the credit from the Revenue;

(*d*) since the payment is made under deduction of tax, it is a charge on the covenantor's income and thus deductible in computing his total income for all income tax purposes (*Howe* v *IRC*). If ICTA 1970, s 457 applies, the payment is a charge at the basic rate only. To the extent that a payment is a charge on income, the covenantor does not bear income tax on it for himself and so gets tax relief.

If the covenantor has insufficient income liable to income tax to cover the payment, ICTA 1970, s 53 will apply. The same procedure is followed but:

(*a*) basic rate tax is deducted at the rate in force in the year in which the payment is made and the recipient is taxed in that year;

(*b*) if the covenantor is an individual, the payment will not be a charge on income (he has insufficient income);

(*c*) the covenantor is required to account to the Inland Revenue for the basic rate deducted. Under ICTA 1970, s 52 there is no such obligation. This is relevant when the covenantor fails to deduct tax (see below).

Example
X is retired and in the tax year 1980/81 only has investment income of £10,000. He makes a covenant of £1,000 pa in favour of his minor grandchild to help pay for her school fees. Assuming the covenant satisfies all the anti-avoidance provisions except ICTA 1970, s 457 and that the grandchild has no other income, the tax position of each will be:

Tax calculation		Grandparent	Grandchild
		£	£
Income		10,000·00	1,000
Less: covenanted sum		1,000·00	
		9,000·00	
Less: personal relief		1,375·00	1,375
Taxable income		7,625·00	nil
Tax: 30% on £7,625		2,287·50	
15% on £3,500*		525·00	
Basic rate on £1,000 (s 52)		300·00	
15% excess liability on £1,000 (s 457)		150·00	
Tax		3,262·50	nil
Financial Position			
Net income		10,000·00	Net c'nant 700
Tax	£3,262·50		Tax cr 300
Net covenant	£700·00	3,962·50	
Available income		6,037·50	1,000

*Personal reliefs do not affect the additional rate tax unless they exceed £5,500.

The excess liability of £150 under ICTA 1970, s 457 is calculated by adding the £1,000 back into the covenantor's income for the higher rate tax calculation (nil, as higher rates start at £11,250 taxable income) and for the additional rate of tax, which produces the 15 per cent rate levied on £1,000.

Overall, the covenant costs the grandparent £700 and the Inland Revenue £300; the grandchild gets £1,000.

4.04 Failure to deduct tax

If the covenantor fails to deduct tax, he cannot normally recover the basic rate from the recipient. Under ICTA 1970, s 52, the Inland Revenue will receive the basic rate tax on the payment from the covenantor, so if the covenantor makes a payment of £1,000 pa, gross, he will have to pay a further £300 to the Inland Revenue. The recipient will be treated as having received a tax free gift of £300 and is taxed on £1,000 with a basic rate tax credit. If ICTA 1970, s 53 applies, the Inland Revenue have the option of recovering the basic rate from the recipient when the covenantor fails to deduct tax, and if they do, no problem arises. Otherwise, under ICTA 1970, s 53 they may recover the basic rate from the covenantor or the person through whom the payment is made and if so, the recipient is taxed on £1,000 with a basic rate tax credit and is treated as having received a tax free gift of £300.

4.05 Free of tax clauses

There are a number of different ways of expressing the amount of the covenanted payments:

£1,000 per annum

The payer will deduct the basic rate of tax for the relevant year; the recipient will receive a net sum and will be taxed on the gross with the basic rate tax credit.

Such sum as after deduction of income tax at the basic rate for the time being in force shall leave £1,000 per annum

This is construed as a covenant for gross payment (£1,428·57 with tax at 30 per cent) which fluctuates with the basic rate of tax. The covenantor deducts basic rate (£428·57 if the rate is 30 per cent) and pays over £1,000. The recipient is taxed on the gross amount with a basic rate tax credit.

£1,000 per annum free of tax

This is construed as a covenant under which the recipient is entitled to end up with £1,000, no more, no less, after having paid tax at all rates. This clause causes a number of difficult problems and should only be used with caution. For a more detailed description of the implications, see White's *Tax Planning on Marriage Breakdown* (Oyez) at p 61.

4.06 Capital transfer tax

A voluntary covenanted payment will be a disposition reducing the value of the covenantor's estate for capital transfer tax, and thus a transfer of value and perhaps a chargeable transfer liable to capital transfer tax at the relevant rates. However, the following exemptions dealt with in Chapter 2 will usually apply and as a result it will be unusual for a charge to capital transfer tax to arise on covenanted payments:

(*a*) dispositions for the maintenance of the family (FA 1975, s 46);

(*b*) the annual £2,000 exemption (FA 1975, Sched 6, para 2);

(*c*) the annual £250 exemption (FA 1975, Sched 6, para 4);

(*d*) the normal expenditure out of income exemption (FA 1975, Sched 6, para 5).

4.07 Tax effective covenants for children and the effect of covenants on grants

Unmarried children under 18

Covenants by a parent in favour of his infant unmarried child are ineffective for income tax purposes and should never be used.

Covenants by any person other than a parent, eg by a grandparent are effective for basic rate tax purposes only. The recipient child will be entitled to a single person's relief and can set this off against his gross income. If the amount of the tax credit exceeds his overall tax liability, the excess may be recovered from the Inland Revenue on production of a tax deduction certificate in form R185. Recovery of the tax credit is usually on an annual basis at the end of the tax year, but arrangements can be made to recover the tax credit more frequently if there is more than one payment in the tax year.

Since the abolition of child relief (except for certain students and overseas children) the receipt of income by a child has no adverse effect on his parents' tax bill. No overall tax advantage will be reaped to the extent that the child pays basic rate tax on the receipt. The covenant should be made in favour of trustees for the benefit of the child or should provide that the receipt of the parent or guardian of the child is sufficient.

The tax and financial consequences are illustrated at p 59.

Adult or married children, including those with grants

ICTA 1970, s 437 does not apply to adult or married children, so parents also can make tax effective covenants in their favour. The tax and financial consequences are the same as non-parental covenants in favour of children under 18 (see above) but educational grants may be affected. A covenantor must be careful to ensure that the covenanted payments do not simply replace money which the local authority would otherwise pay as a grant; not only is that a waste of the covenantor's money but also of the recipient's tax reliefs since unlike covenanted payments, grants are not liable to income tax.

The basic rules are that a student is entitled to a grant for:

(*a*) fees for admission, tuition and exams; and

(*b*) maintenance; it is this part of the grant only which can be affected by covenants.

The amount of the maintenance grant is the difference between the student's requirements (which are laid down and vary from course to course) and his resources, and is subject to a minimum of £385 for the year 1980/81. Resources include:

(*a*) his income in excess of £310 for the year 1980/81, disregarding vacation earnings and parental covenants (not others) if the parent is expected to contribute to his maintenance;

(*b*) the parental contribution, established by applying a formula to his parents' residual income, ie income after deductions for commitments such as mortgage interest but no deduction is given for covenanted payments in favour of the child.

Thus, if a parent makes a covenant in favour of his adult or married child, it will not affect the amount required as a parental contribution and equally it will not reduce the grant to the child. A parent can, therefore, safely covenant to pay the amount of the parental covenant or more, without adverse effect on the grant, unless the student is over 24 years of age (see below).

A covenant by any other person is taken into account in assessing the student's resources and is, therefore, financially ineffective unless:

(*a*) the student is already on a minimum maintenance grant; or

(*b*) to the extent the covenant does not exceed £310 pa if the student has no other income which he has to take into account; or

(*c*) if the covenant is to take the place of the contribution the parent would otherwise be expected to make.

For mature students – those over 24 years of age – no parental contribution is required and all covenanted payments will be taken into account in assessing his resources (with the first £310 income per annum disregarded as before).

Use of covenants to pay life assurance premiums

Where basic rate tax relief has been given to a covenanted sum, further tax relief can be obtained by using the payments to pay the premiums on a life assurance policy on the life of the recipient. This can be very valuable to the recipient. For example, if the net sum covenanted is £100 (the cost to the covenantor), the basic rate tax credit is £42·86 (with tax at 30 per cent). If this £142·86 is paid as a premium net of life assurance relief (at present 17½ per cent), the gross premium with the tax relief, is £173·16. The Inland Revenue, therefore, contribute to the premiums over 73 per cent of what the covenantor contributes. Life assurance relief reduces to 15 per cent in 1981/82.

No life assurance relief will be given to a child of "tender years" (ie under 12 years of age) who takes out a policy on his own life since the child cannot be considered capable of making the contract in the first place. However, relief will be given to such a child if the policy on his life is first taken out by another with an insurable interest, eg a parent, and is then assigned to the child (see Inland Revenue Statements of Practice SP 4/79 and SP 11/79, dated 28 February 1979 and 1 November 1979 respectively).

The proceeds of such policies can be used to provide a valuable capital sum, for example to pay school fees (see p 66).

Chapter 5

SCHOOL FEES

Every parent wants to have his children educated in the best possible manner; many feel that private education is the answer and then spend many years struggling to find the money to pay the school fees. School fees can be met in a number of ways and the best choice can save a considerable amount of money. This Chapter looks at the more important ways in which school fees can be provided and considers the tax and financial effect of each.

5.01 Out of pocket payments

Payment of school fees may be on an *ad hoc* basis, the fees being met as and when they arise, either out of income or out of capital. There is no fiscal or financial advantage in paying in this way. If paid out of income, no income tax relief is given. If paid out of capital, it may be necessary to sell assets to realise sufficient to pay the fees, in which case capital gains tax must be considered.

If the fees are paid by a parent, no capital transfer tax will arise since the payment of school fees is within FA 1975, s 46, dispositions for the maintenance of the family, which exempts dispositions made by one party to a marriage in favour of a child of either party which are for the maintenance, education or training of the child for a period ending not later than the year in which the child attains the age of 18 or, if later, ceases to undergo full-time education or training (see p 26).

If the fees are paid by someone other than the child's parents, FA 1975, s 46 will not apply unless the child is not in the care of his parents but for substantial periods has been in the care of the payer (FA 1975, s 46(2)). The non-gratuitous exemption under FA 1975, s 20(4) will not apply since the payer is gratuitously providing education for the child, but other exemptions should cover the payment, such as the normal expenditure out of income exemption and the £2,000 and £250 annual exemptions.

5.02 Paying school fees by deed of covenant

Payments under a deed of covenant in favour of a child may be used to pay his school fees. Deeds of covenant are dealt with comprehensively in Chapter 4; to summarise, a covenant in favour of the covenantor's infant unmarried child is ineffective for income tax purposes, but other covenants are usually effective for basic rate tax purposes only and this provides a fiscal advantage provided the child himself does not have to bear the basic rate of tax on the payments.

If the covenant is started well in advance of the time when the liability for school fees arises, the payments under the covenant can be invested in endowment policies on the life of the child, maturing at the appropriate times, the premiums on which qualify for life assurance relief. The policy cannot be taken out by a child of tender years (under 12 years of age), so if he is under this age, it must be taken out by his parent and the benefit assigned to him to ensure that life assurance relief is given on the payment of the premiums by the child.

A covenant by a third person, eg a grandparent, in favour of the parents, rather than the child, to enable them to pay school fees, has no fiscal advantage if the husband is taxed at the basic rate also. Whether the covenant is in favour of the husband or the wife, if they are living together, the receipt will be treated as the investment income of the husband, regardless of an election for separate taxation.

A covenant in favour of the school will be the income of the school for income tax purposes and, being a covenant in return for schooling, will not be pure income profit in the hands of the school and thus not an annual payment (see p 55). This means that the payer gets no tax relief for the covenanted payments and should make them gross. Such covenants, therefore, have the same effect as out of pocket payments of school fees.

The capital transfer tax consequences of deeds of covenant are dealt with on p 61.

5.03 Employer based schemes

There are two main ways in which employers have provided for the education of their employees' children. The first is by setting up a trust for the education of the employees' children which involves no selection procedure (see *Ball* v *National and Grindlays Bank* [1973] Ch 127). Such a trust will not be charitable since it confers no public benefit (*Oppenheim* v *Tobacco Securities Trust* [1951] AC 297) and no tax relief will be given to the employer for his contributions to the trust. When school fees are paid, they are treated as the income of the child (*Barclays Bank Ltd* v *Naylor* [1961] Ch 7) and not of the parent, but since FA 1976, if the employee is a director or highly paid employee (for 1980/81, earning £8,500 pa or more including the value of benefits in kind), the amount of the payment of school fees by the employer will be a benefit in kind taxable under Schedule E in the employee's hands (FA 1976, ss 61, 63 and 72(3)). There is, therefore, no fiscal advantage in paying school fees in this way except to an employee who is not a director nor highly paid; it will not be tax advantageous to the employer who could produce the same result simply by paying the school fees direct.

The second way is for the employer to set up a scheme involving a selection procedure; the scheme could well involve the creation of a charitable trust (eg *IRC* v *Educa-*

tional Grants Association [1967] Ch 123 and 993) and if so, the contributions to it by the employer, would be deductible if made by covenant. The income of the charitable trust would be exempt if applicable to charitable purposes only and if applied to charitable purposes only (ICTA 1970, s 360(1)(*c*)); this means that the public must receive a substantial benefit, so the set-up becomes philanthropic. The receipt of income is scholarship income in the hands of the child and therefore exempt from income tax under ICTA 1970, s 375, which provides that income from a scholarship (including an exhibition, bursary or any other similar educational endowment) held by a person receiving full-time education at a university, college, school or other educational establishment shall be exempt from income tax. However, although the child is not taxed, the parent will usually be taxed if he is a director or highly paid employee, following an Inland Revenue Statement dated 14 June 1978 (and supplemented by a Statement dated 20 June 1978), the main parts of which are:

> "2. The Revenue are now advised that ICTA 1970, s 375, whilst exempting from tax the scholarship income in the scholar's hands, does not prevent the cost of providing the scholarship from being a benefit taxable under FA 1976, s 61. They therefore propose in future to contend for liability under that section, and in accordance with FA 1976, s 72(3) where a scholarship is awarded to a member of the family or household of a director or higher paid employee and the award is made by reason of the latter's employment. Thus where an employer sets up and finances an arrangement under which awards are made to the children of directors or higher-paid employees, the Revenue will contend that those awards give rise to benefits provided by reason of the employment and are therefore assessable on the parents.
>
> 3. The Revenue will not, however, contend that there is a benefit giving rise to liability under FA 1976, s 61 where there is only a fortuitous connection between the identity of the recipient of the scholarship and his parent's employment, for example where a firm sets up a scheme for awarding scholarships which is open to all, but where one of the successful candidates happens to be the child of a higher-paid employee of that firm."

"Open to all" means open to the public at large.

There are also on the market artificial employer-based schemes where, it is stated, the employers' contributions are tax deductible and no tax is levied on the employee, regardless of status, nor on the child. The effect of such schemes remains a matter of doubt and independent and informed legal advice must always be taken before such schemes are purchased.

5.04 Composition schemes

Some private schools run schemes under which fees can be paid in advance by means of a reduced lump sum. The schemes vary considerably from school to school. For example, one school has a scheme under which a parent can pay in advance for twelve terms of education and is then given a thirteenth term, free. Other schemes simply give a straightforward discount based on the interest the school would earn on the lump sum if invested. Generally, likely increases in the fees will be taken into account, but the parent will nevertheless be liable to pay any increase not already provided for.

If the chosen school runs a composition fee scheme, it could well be more financially attractive than commercial school fees schemes (see below) and the alternatives must be compared carefully.

5.05 Insured schemes

A number of commercial organisations, particularly Life Assurance Companies have produced various plans to help with the payment of school fees. These include:

Endowment assurance scheme

This involves the payment of premiums on suitably maturing with profits endowment policies. Life assurance relief will be given if the policy is on the life of the person paying the premiums, the relief being that the premiums are payable under deduction of 17½ per cent for 1980/81

(15 per cent for 1981/82 onwards) provided all premiums payable by the taxpayer on qualifying policies do not exceed the greater of one-sixth of the taxpayer's total income and £1,500.

If no benefit is taken from the policy within 7 years of its creation, no tax liability arises on maturity; if a benefit is taken within this period of time, a higher rate tax liability can arise.

School fees spreading scheme

A second type of scheme enables the parent to spread the payment of school fees over a period longer than the duration of the child's schooling. Payments by the parent under the scheme can be covered by life assurance and are usually started well in advance of the date when the child starts school. Such schemes save little and are not usually financially advantageous. One scheme gives an example of the saving for a 35 year old father who wishes to provide fees of £2,000 a year for 5 years, for his 10 year old daughter who will start schooling in 3 years time. Fees total £10,000 but the cost under the scheme is £9,400, a saving of £600 only. There are no fiscal benefits in such a scheme, except in so far as the life assurance premiums qualify for relief.

School fees capital scheme

Schemes exist whereby a capital sum is paid to an educational trust, which invests the money with a Life Assurance Company to produce the school fees when required. If the money is provided by the parent, no further tax liability should arise, but there is a possibility of capital transfer tax if the money is provided by another.

The saving under such a scheme is not great. A careful selection of appropriately maturing gilts (see below) can produce a better return and it is even possible to invest the money in a Building Society and do better. For example, if fees of £2,000 a year are to be provided immediately for the next 5 years, a school fees capital scheme would require a lump sum of £8,338 immediately, a saving of £1,662. Compare this with what can be done with gilts (see below).

5.06 The gilts scheme

The gilts scheme is one of the more financially effective ways of providing school fees out of a cash lump sum. The way it works is:

(*a*) work out precisely when the school fees are required;

(*b*) buy a selection of gilts which mature at the right time to pay the required sums each year;

(*c*) use the income from the gilts to take out an endowment policy which with life assurance relief on the premiums, should produce a reasonable capital sum on maturity, reimbursing some of the capital expenditure on the school fees.

A comparison between this scheme and the school fees capital scheme is illustrated in the following Example.

Example

£2,000 pa school fees are to be provided immediately for the next 5 years. Gilts may be chosen as follows:

Gilt	*Maturing*	*Price*	*Cost to buy £2,000 worth*	*Income*
Exchequer 3%	1981	£93⅛	£1,863	60
Treasury 3%	1982	£90	£1,800	120
Exchequer "A" 3%	1983	£82¾	£1,655	180
Exchequer 3%	1984	£74¾	£1,495	240
			£6,813	£600

The first £2,000 could be invested in a very short dated gilt (without tax relief on maturity), to show some profit. The gain made on the listed gilts will be capital gains tax free if held for more than a year.

No capital transfer tax will be payable by a parent using the scheme since the payment of school fees will be within FA 1975, s 46, dispositions for the maintenance of the family. For others using this scheme the normal expenditure out of income exemption would not apply since the payments will not be out of income, but the annual exemptions of £2,000 and £250 should apply.

5.07 On marriage breakdown

Marriage breakdown is dealt with in Chapter 6, but one small consolation which can result is the opportunity it provides for a tax efficient method of paying school fees by the parents. This arises because the Inland Revenue do not consider payments made direct to a person under a court order to be settlements within the anti-avoidance provisions in ICTA 1970, ss 434–459. This does not apply if the order creates a trust (see *Yates* v *Starkey* 1951 Ch 465).

This means that payments direct to a child under a court order on marriage breakdown, are fully effective for all income tax purposes, and an order to pay school fees to the child, qualifies. The written receipt of the parent with custody will be stated to be sufficient. Furthermore, the court may order payments to be made direct to the school instead, with the same tax effect since the payment will be made to the school as agent for the child, unlike a covenant with the school, which is a contract with the school and which is tax-ineffective. In *Court Business*, 11 January 1980, published by the Lord Chancellor's department, the following passage appears:

> "*Payment of School Fees*
>
> It sometimes arises that a father is ordered to make periodical payments in respect of his children which include an element on account of school fees.
>
> Courts will wish to know that an arrangement has recently been made with the Inland Revenue whereby school fees may be paid directly to the school and tax relief will be allowed on the part of the payment made in respect of them if the order directing payment contains the formula:
>
> > 'that that part of the order which reflects the school fees shall be paid to the [headmaster] [bursar] [school secretary] as agent for the said child and the receipt of the payee shall be a sufficient discharge'."

The school fees will be the income of the child for income tax purposes whether paid to the child or to the school direct.

5.08 Accumulation and maintenance settlements

Accumulation and maintenance settlements are dealt with in detail in Chapter 3 but mention of them must be made again here because they can be used to provide a fund out of which a child's school fees can be met. If the fees are met out of the income of the settlement, they will be treated as the child's income. If they are met out of capital, no capital transfer tax liability will arise. The disadvantages of accumulation and maintenance settlements are:

(*a*) they cannot generally be used by parents to create a fund for school fees because of ICTA 1970, s 437 (see p 34).

(*b*) for others, the creation of the settlement can give rise to a capital transfer tax and capital gains tax liability.

Nevertheless, if a settlement is created by a third party, use of the income or capital for school fees is fiscally and financially neutral.

5.09 Private education on the state

It should never be forgotten that the state can, at its discretion, sometimes help with boarding school fees. The most common case where this happens is where the parents are overseas or they move around this country too frequently to enable their children to attend day school for any length of time. Other cases include:

(*a*) the child shows a special aptitude requiring boarding school training;

(*b*) family circumstances make a boarding education inevitable or desirable;

(*c*) the child cannot get a suitable education except at a boarding school.

Full details of these discretionary awards can be obtained from Local Education Offices.

Chapter 6

MARRIAGE BREAKDOWN

6.01 Generally

Having children can make the misfortune of marriage breakdown more bitter, but out of that misfortune some small comfort may be gained in the tax advantages which can be derived from careful planning of the benefits to be distributed among those involved. This Chapter deals primarily with the tax position of children on marriage breakdown and shows what tax savings and pitfalls there are. Financial provision for a recipient spouse is not dealt with except in connection with the matrimonial home where the children will continue to reside. For a comprehensive coverage of the tax and financial implications of marriage breakdown, readers are recommended *Tax Planning on Marriage Breakdown* written by the author of this work, and published by Oyez.

6.02 Maintenance for children

Financial provision must be made for dependent children when the parties to a marriage separate or divorce, and this will usually take the form of maintenance through periodical payments. This can be done in three different ways:

(*a*) by a purely voluntary or domestic arrangement;
(*b*) by a maintenance or separation agreement;
(*c*) under a court order.

Each of these alternatives will be considered in turn.

Voluntary maintenance

The essence of voluntary maintenance is that no legally binding obligation is created. No court order or binding agreement will exist and the payments must be made under a purely domestic arrangement; if so they are regarded as gifts for income tax purposes and thus outside the income tax net. The income tax consequences of voluntary maintenance for a child, regardless of whether the payments are made to the other party to the marriage for the benefit of the child or to the child direct, are:

(*a*) the recipient is not taxed on the income;
(*b*) the paying spouse gets no tax relief for the maintenance payments and makes them without deducting tax;
(*c*) a paying husband will qualify for married man's relief if he can show that his wife is wholly maintained by him and the payments do not qualify for tax relief (ICTA 1970, s 8); this will increase his personal reliefs by £770 for the tax year 1980/81.

If the money received for a child is not wholly used up in maintenance, the income produced by any balance invested for the child will be treated as that of the payer, if the child is his infant unmarried child (see ICTA 1970, s 437 and *Thomas* v *Marshall* [1953] AC 543).

Voluntary maintenance for a child should be exempt from capital transfer tax as a disposition for the maintenance of the family (FA 1975, s 46), or within the exemptions for normal expenditure out of income, the £2,000 and £250 exemptions (FA 1975, Sched 6, paras 2, 4 and 5).

Maintenance or separation agreements

Payments made under a valid maintenance or separation agreement will be made under a legally binding obligation and if made to or for the benefit of the infant unmarried child of the payer, will be a settlement within ICTA 1970, s 437 (see p 56). If ICTA 1970, s 437 applies, the payments remain the income of the payer for all income tax purposes and he pays gross; the recipient is not taxed. The effect is, therefore, exactly the same as for voluntary maintenance but under ICTA 1970, s 441, the payer may recover from the recipient the extra tax he has to pay as a result of ICTA 1970, s 437; clearly if this right is exercised the child would suffer a very serious disadvantage and a maintenance of separation agreement for an infant unmarried child must be avoided.

If payments are to be made for such a child, they must be made to the recipient parent direct without mention of the child, in which case full tax relief is given for the paying spouse and the recipient spouse is taxed normally on the receipt (which is not treated as investment income), with a credit for the basic rate of tax which will have been deducted under ICTA 1970, ss 52 or 53.

Maintenance or separation agreements providing periodical payments for the payer's adult or married child will not be caught by ICTA 1970, s 437 and the tax effect is the same as for a covenant (see p 59).

Court orders

Under the Matrimonial Causes Act 1973, s 23 the court has power to order periodical payments, secured or unsecured, in favour of a child of the family, but by MCA 1973, s 29, no order may be made in favour of a child who has reached the age of 18 and periodical payments may not continue beyond a child's eighteenth birthday unless in either case, eg the child is receiving instruction at an educational establishment or undergoing training for a trade, profession or vocation. There are three ways in which the court might exercise this power:

PAYMENTS TO A SPOUSE FOR THE BENEFIT OF THE CHILD

Payments may be ordered to be made to by one party to the marriage to the other for the maintenance of the child. These are treated as the income of the spouse and not that of the child (*Stevens* v *Tirard* [1939] 2 KB 410) and ICTA 1970, s 437 does not apply; full tax relief will, therefore, be given to the paying spouse and the recipient will be taxed normally on the receipt (which is not investment income) with a credit for the basic rate of tax deducted. Payments under a court order to a spouse which are small maintenance payments (£33 per week or £143 per month) are paid gross, but nevertheless qualify the payer for tax relief and are otherwise taxed normally.

PAYMENTS TO A SPOUSE ON TRUST FOR THE CHILD

If the court order creates a trust for an infant unmarried child, ICTA 1970, s 437 applies and the payments are totally ineffective for all income tax purposes (*Yates* v *Starkey* (1951) Ch 465). Such orders should be avoided.

PAYMENTS DIRECT TO THE CHILD

The court has power to order payments direct to a child (or to a school on behalf of the child, see p 72) and the receipt of the parent or guardian (or bursar) will be ordered to be sufficient. Such payments are not considered by the Inland Revenue to be settlements and are thus outside ICTA 1970, s 437 (and presumably ICTA 1970, s 457). The income tax consequences of this are:

(*a*) the payer will be given full income tax relief for the payments; the virtual abolition of child relief means that there is no consequent loss of personal relief;

(*b*) if the payments are small maintenance payments (for a child, up to £18 per week or £78 per month) they are made gross; otherwise they are made under deduction of basic rate tax (which the Revenue will in due course collect);

(*c*) the child will be taxed normally on the gross income, setting off, for example, personal reliefs and if the payments are received net the tax credit may be recovered;

(*d*) the payments are not the investment income of the child (FA 1974, s 15 and FA 1978, s 21).

Capital transfer tax and court orders

The Inland Revenue apparently take the view that payments under a court order are within the non-gratuitous exemption (FA 1975, s 20(4)) so long as there is no gratuitous intent (see the statement, p 80). If there is gratuitous intent, the normal exemptions should apply, eg dispositions for the maintenance of the family, the £2,000 and £250 exemptions and the normal expenditure out of income exemption.

Secured periodical payments

It may well be desirable to provide security for periodical payments made under a court order, to ensure that a child will continue to benefit even though the payer may be disinclined to continue the payments. The usual order for securing (see *Shearn* v *Shearn* [1931] P 1) can cause serious capital transfer tax difficulties and an alternative method of securing payments using two parallel orders, should be used (see Potter and Monroe, *Tax Planning with Precedents*, 8th ed, pp 57–60 and White, *Tax Planning on Marriage Breakdown*, pp 96 and 97).

What arrangements for maintenance of a child should be made?

VOLUNTARY MAINTENANCE

The main advantage of voluntary maintenance is that the recipient is not taxed. Such maintenance is however a waste of the recipient's personal relief and confers no tax advantage on the payer (except the possible claim for an extra £770 personal relief) and should, therefore, be avoided.

MAINTENANCE OR SEPARATION AGREEMENTS

Because of ICTA 1970, s 437, payments made under a maintenance or separation agreement to or for the benefit of the payer's infant unmarried child will be treated in the same way as voluntary maintenance and there is no tax advantage. If the payments are included in the amounts paid to a recipient spouse (without reference to the child), the payer will be given tax relief, but the recipient spouse will receive them under deduction of tax and will be taxed on them.

Payments to an adult or married child are not caught by ICTA 1970, s 437, but are ineffective for excess liability purposes (ICTA 1970, s 437).

COURT ORDERS

Because a court order for payments direct to a child is not regarded by the Inland Revenue as a settlement, payments to a child are fully effective for all income tax purposes, enabling the child to use up personal reliefs and other deductions; the payer is given full tax relief for the payments. A cash flow advantage can be obtained if the payments are small maintenance payments.

Orders on trust for the child should be avoided and payments direct to the spouse for the benefit of the child simply waste the child's personal reliefs and deductions.

6.03 Capital provision for children

Although there may well be a tax advantage in transferring property to, or settling property on a child, it is unusual for a court to exercise its powers under the Matrimonial Causes Act 1973, s 24 to make a property transfer order or settlement order, unless the order is a consent order following agreement between the parties. However, transfers of property or settlements for children should always be considered on marriage breakdown; the tax effect of outright transfers is dealt with in Chapter 2 and children's settlements are covered in Chapter 3. In addition to the capital transfer tax consequences dealt with in those two Chapters, where a court order is involved, it may be that the disposition is within the non-gratuitous exemption in FA 1975, s 20(4) and is thus not a transfer of value. The Senior Registrar of the Family Division with the agreement of the Inland Revenue, issued this statement in 1975 ((1975) 119 SJ 596):

> "Transfers of money or property pursuant to an order of the Court in consequence of a decree of divorce or nullity will, in general, be regarded as exempt from capital transfer tax as transactions at arm's length which are not intended to confer any gratuitous benefit. If, exceptionally, such a benefit is intended it is the duty of the transferor to deliver a capital transfer tax account to the Capital Taxes Office."

6.04 The matrimonial home

Generally

Young children need a roof over their heads; on marriage breakdown, this will usually be the former matrimonial home and the problem is how to arrange the property interests in the home not only to protect the interests of the children but also to best tax and financial advantage for both parties to the marriage.

Capital gains tax

The problem with rearrangements of interests in the matrimonial home is mainly capital gains tax (although, as will be seen, capital transfer tax has a part to play). The relevant rules are:

HUSBAND AND WIFE

While husband and wife are living together, transfers between them are deemed to have been made at a consideration which gives rise to neither gain nor loss, thus postponing any potential capital gains tax liability. Once the spouses separate, this relief is lost and transfers between them will be deemed to have been made at market value at the date of the transfer. Subject to the private dwelling house exemption and Extra-Statutory Concession D6, below, any gain deemed to have been made will be liable to tax at 30 per cent, although the first £3,000 of an individual's chargeable gains in the tax year, are exempt. Further, by FA 1980, s 79, gains made on transactions between individuals not at arm's length can be held over if both parties jointly elect to so do.

PRIVATE DWELLING HOUSE EXEMPTION

The matrimonial home itself will be within the private dwelling house exemption if it was the only or main residence of the spouse disposing his interest, provided he occupied it throughout his period of ownership, ignoring the last 24 months. Certain other periods of absence are also ignored (see CGTA 1979, ss 101, 102 and FA 1980, s 80). If the transfer of the interest in the matrimonial home takes place over 24 months after the transferring spouse left it, a time apportioned part of the gain will be chargeable, subject to ESC D6 below.

EXTRA-STATUTORY CONCESSION D6

Where a married couple separate or divorce and one ceases to occupy the matrimonial home and subsequently as part of a financial settlement disposes of the home, or an interest in it, to the other, the private dwelling-house exemption will continue to apply up to the date of transfer provided the other spouse continues to use the home as an only or main residence and the disposing spouse has not elected that some other house should be treated as his only or main residence. Clearly it is better to make the transfer within 2 years after separation if the spouse who left the home has another property eligible for relief; if use is made of ESC D6 a proportionate amount of the relief is lost in respect of the new house.

Capital transfer tax

On marriage breakdown, transfers between spouses will be within the spouse exemption until decree absolute. Thereafter the non-gratuitous exemption in FA 1975, s 20(4) may well apply (see the Statement of the Senior Registrar of the Family Division, above), or failing that, possibly FA 1975, s 46 (dispositions for the maintenance of the family).

Outright transfer of interest

The capital gains tax and capital transfer tax rules (see above) apply if one party transfers outright to the other party the whole or part of his interest in the matrimonial home. If some interest is retained by the absent spouse, on a subsequent disposal capital gains tax will be leviable, relief being given for the period of occupation before marriage breakdown.

Outright transfer of interest subject to charge

On an outright transfer, the parties may agree or the court may order that the transferring spouse should be given a charge on the house for a specified sum or a percentage of the equity, with payment of the sum charged to be postponed, eg until the earlier of the death of either spouse, the sale of the house or the attaining of a specified age by the youngest child. If the charge is for a specified sum, no further capital tax liability arises when it is paid; if the charge is for a percentage of the equity, it would appear that a capital gains tax charge could arise when the sum is paid (see *Marson* v *Marriage* [1980] STC 177).

Despite this, a percentage sum is financially much more valuable than the specified sum.

Postponed sales

Whether or not beneficial interests are varied, if both spouses retain some interest in the matrimonial home, the court may order that sale should be postponed, eg until the youngest child reaches 17 (see *Mesher* v *Mesher* [1980] 1 All ER 126). When the sale takes place, capital gains tax will be leviable on the interest of the absent spouse, private dwelling-house relief being given for his period of occupation before marriage breakdown.

Settlements of the matrimonial home

It can be fiscally and financially more advantageous if the matrimonial home is settled, eg on the occupying spouse for life or, if earlier, until the youngest child reaches 18, with remainder to both spouses equally. This is a settlement for capital gains tax and capital transfer tax. If it is created within 2 years of separation, no capital gains tax will be levied then, as a result of the private dwelling-house exemption, and normal capital transfer tax rules apply. Despite the interest in remainder of the absent spouse, the private residence exemption will apply on the disposal by the trustees of the home because it is occupied by a beneficiary of a settlement (CGTA 1979, s 104). Thus if the absent spouse is alive when the settlement comes to an end, he will receive his share free of capital gains tax, and, because of the reverter to settlor exemption in FA 1975, Sched 5, para 4(5), free of capital transfer tax. No capital gains tax or capital transfer tax will be payable by the occupying spouse either. This is undoubtedly the most financially and fiscally attractive method of dealing with the matrimonial home, but serious capital transfer tax problems arise if the absent spouse dies before the life interest terminates (see White, *Tax Planning on Marriage Breakdown* (Oyez), p 139) and this possibility must be carefully considered before a settlement is made.

Mortgage interest

Income tax relief for mortgage interest paid in respect of the former matrimonial home is given by FA 1974,

Sched 1, para 4 only to the payer, and to the extent of his estate or interest therein, up to the statutory limit of £25,000 for all qualifying loans. Additionally, on marriage breakdown the Inland Revenue give the relief to the occupying spouse who pays the mortgage interest regardless of ownership of the home (see the Inland Revenue Pamphlet *Income Tax, Separation and Divorce*, IR 30 at p 6).

If the absent spouse pays the interest, relief will be limited to the size of his estate or interest in the home and may also be restricted by the £25,000 limit, particularly if he owns another home. These difficulties can be circumvented by arranging for the occupying spouse to pay the mortgage interest and for the absent spouse to put her in funds to do so by increasing maintenance. In this way the absent spouse receives unlimited relief for the extra maintenance and the occupying spouse will be given the mortgage interest relief to offset against the increased maintenance. However, cash flow problems will arise if maintenance is paid under deduction of tax and it may be necessary for the absent spouse to compensate for this, eg by lending the amount of the basic rate tax credit to the other pending recovery from the Inland Revenue.

Married Women's Property Act 1882, s 17

The court has power to declare what beneficial rights already exist in relation to property, including the matrimonial home. If those rights differ from the manner in which the legal estate is held, eg, because of substantial contributions to the improvement of the home made by one party, no tax or stamp duty liability arises when the legal estate is transferred in accordance with those rights. If, on the other hand, a property transfer order is used under MCA 1973, s 24 to give effect to those rights, unless the Inland Revenue can be persuaded that those rights did in fact already exist, stamp duty and, possibly, capital gains tax could be leviable. Thus, before embarking on an application for a property transfer order, consider first the possibility of an application under MWPA 1882, s 17.

Chapter 7

PASSING DOWN THE FAMILY BUSINESS: PARTNERSHIPS WITH CHILDREN

7.01 The capital tax problem

An impressive array of tax reliefs mitigate the burden of capital taxes on gifts and sales of interests in family businesses, but despite this, the capital tax burden on passing down the family business to the next generation (or direct to the third generation) can be overwhelming. For example, a £500,000 controlling interest in a business with 50 per cent business relief will cost a minimum of £104,000 in capital transfer tax if given away on death or £69,000 on a lifetime gift, assuming the donee pays tax. In the latter case there is also a potential 30 per cent capital gains tax charge which may be postponed. Although capital transfer tax could be paid by instalments, this capital tax burden could easily cripple the financial position of those taking over the business, forcing a sale out of the family. Rather than simply resting on the reliefs given by statute, therefore, it may well be necessary to take further planning steps to bring the capital tax burden within manageable limits.

The general principles for gifts to children are dealt with in Chapter 2. The purpose of this Chapter is to suggest a number of ways in which the capital tax burden on businesses can be mitigated where a limited company is not involved. The tax efficient use of the reliefs is fundamental to this, so they will be dealt with first.

7.02 The capital transfer tax reliefs

Business property relief (FA 1976, Sched 10 (as amended))

The value transferred by a transfer of value is reduced by an appropriate percentage, to the extent that the transfer is attributable to relevant business property, as follows:

Relevant business property	*Percentage reduction*
(*a*) A business or an interest in a business.	50%
(*b*) A controlling interest in shares or securities in a company (including part of a controlling interest held jointly by spouses).	50%
(*c*) A non-controlling interest in an unquoted company.	20%
(*d*) Land or buildings, machinery or plant which immediately before the transfer was used wholly or mainly for the purposes of a business carried on by a company which the transferor then had control or by a partnership of which he then was a partner (ie property owned personally by the transferor).	30%

Business includes profession and vocation but not a business carried on otherwise than for gain and no relief is given if the interest involved is deemed not to be relevant business property, for example:

(*a*) where the business, or the business of the company, consists wholly or mainly of one or more of dealing in securities, stocks or shares, land or buildings or making or holding investments. Shares in holding companies are relevant business property if the businesses of subsidiaries are not within this paragraph;

(*b*) where what would otherwise be relevant business property is under a contract for sale or the company is in the process of being wound up. Here the assets are, in effect, cash, so no relief is given;

(*c*) where the transferor has not owned the property throughout the 2 preceding years or, if the property replaced other property, it and the other property were

not owned by the transferor for at least 2 in the last 5 years;
(*d*) to the extent that the value relates to an asset which was not used wholly or mainly for business purposes for the preceding 2 years, or is not required for future business use.

Agricultural relief (FA 1975, Sched 8 (as amended))

Where the value transferred by a chargeable transfer is determined by reference to the value of agricultural property, if the person liable to pay the tax so claims, the agricultural value of the property is reduced by 50 per cent. The non-agricultural value of the property attracts no relief.

Agricultural property means agricultural land or pasture and includes woodlands if occupied with agricultural land or pasture and the occupation is ancillary to that of the agricultural land or pasture; and also includes such cottages, farm buildings and farm houses, together with the land occupied with them, as are of a character appropriate to the property (FA 1975, Sched 8, para 7). Agricultural property does not, therefore, include livestock and plant and machinery.

Agricultural value means the value of the property if it were subject to a perpetual covenant prohibiting its use otherwise than as agricultural property. No "hope value" or development value is included.

There are a number of strict requirements to satisfy before relief is given for example:
(*a*) the transferor must be a full time working farmer, as defined in FA 1975, Sched 8, para 3 (which includes those undergoing full time education);
(*b*) the land must have been occupied by him (or his company) for agricultural purposes usually throughout the 2 years immediately preceding the transfer;
(*c*) relief is limited to any transferor, to a total of agricultural value of £250,000 and a total area of 1,000 acres, whichever is greater.

Shares in a farming company are treated as agricultural property provided, *inter alia*, they are a controlling interest.

Interaction of business property relief with agricultural relief

No business property relief is given to the extent that the value transferred is reduced under the agricultural relief provisions. To the extent that agricultural relief is not given, eg plant and machinery, livestock, the value of the land in excess of its agricultural value and minority interests in companies, business property relief can be claimed. If no claim for agricultural relief is made, business property relief can be used in full instead. Where both reliefs are available, certain factors may influence choice:

(*a*) business property relief is given by reducing the value transferred by a transfer of value (ie before exemptions), whereas agricultural relief is given by reducing the value transferred by a chargeable transfer (ie after exemptions).

Example
A field is worth £10,000 and is to be given by a father to his son. It qualifies for both reliefs, in full. The father has available an annual exemption of £4,000. If agricultural relief is claimed the value transferred by the chargeable transfer will be £10,000 – £4,000 = £6,000. This is reduced by 50 per cent so the value transferred will be £3,000. If business property relief is claimed, the transfer of value is 50 per cent of £10,000 = £5,000 and the chargeable transfer is £5,000 – £4,000 = £1,000.

(*b*) if the transferor owns the property personally but it is occupied by the company he controls or by a partnership of which he is a member, business property relief is limited to 30 per cent. Agricultural relief is still 50 per cent.

Tax by instalments

Tax may be payable by instalments on certain types of asset including shares and businesses (see p 17). The relief applies also to transfers on death.

7.03 The capital gains tax reliefs

As mentioned on p 16, capital gains tax is not payable on death and there is a new hold-over relief in FA 1980 on gifts between individuals. The old hold-over relief for gifts of business assets in CGTA 1979, s 126 still applies to gifts into settlement (although probably not to gifts to companies).

In addition, capital gains tax relief is given by CGTA 1979, s 124 to an individual who has reached the age of 60 and who disposes by way of sale or gift the whole or part of his business or shares or securities in his family trading company of which he is a full-time working director. A family company is defined as one where the individual owns not less than 25 per cent of the voting rights, or if he owns not less than 5 per cent of the voting rights, he and his family own not less than 51 per cent of the voting rights.

The company must be a trading company, so that shares in a holding company do not qualify for relief. The relief, therefore, ignores the commercial reality of group structures. The relief is that chargeable gains are reduced by up to £10,000 pa for every year by which the individual's age exceeds 60, to a maximum of £50,000. If the individual owned the asset for less than 10 years, there is a percentage reduction in the relief.

Relief is only given to the extent that the assets involved in the business or company are chargeable business assets, ie basically those used for the purposes of the business. The relief is called "Transfer of business on retirement", but there is no requirement that the transferor should actually retire.

Tax may also be payable by instalments (see p 17).

7.04 Taking a child into partnership

The capital tax position of partnerships remains a matter of some debate particularly in relation to capital gains tax, although guidance on this tax has been given by the Inland Revenue in a Statement of Practice dated 17 January 1975 ("the Statement").

A considerable amount of capital tax can be saved if a father takes his child into the business at an early stage rather than wait until death or retirement before handing it over. The capital tax consequences depend on the nature of the interest acquired by the child and the consequent loss to the parents' estate. They will also depend on whether, for capital transfer tax purposes, the transaction is a commercial arrangement, which, although it reduces the value of the parents' estate, is one to which the non-gratuitous exemption under FA 1975, s 20(4) applies. This provides that a disposition is not a transfer of value if it is shown:

(*a*) that there was no intent to confer any gratuitous benefit; and

(*b*) that the transaction was at arm's length between unconnected persons or was on arm's length terms.

Whether or not this exemption applies in any case depends on the facts and the nature of the bargain, but it is inevitable that in any transaction between parent and child, the parties will be very hard pressed to persuade the Inland Revenue that no gratuitous intent was involved if the estate of the parent is diminished. The test seems to be: would the parent have taken an unconnected third person into partnership on the same terms?

The child acquires a profit share only

If the parent takes his child into partnership and gives the child a share in the income profits only, with no immediate right to share in the capital (including the goodwill and surplus on dissolution), provided the work which the child is to carry out is reasonable in view of the reward to be obtained, no capital transfer tax nor capital gains tax will be involved. From a capital transfer tax point of view, any loss to the parents' estate is counteracted by the work required of the child. Capital gains tax is only leviable if a person acquires a share in the surplus assets on winding up (see paras 4 and 7 of the Statement).

The child acquires an interest in the partnership capital

Where the child acquires a share in the surplus assets on dissolution, unless FA 1975, s 20(4) applies, the parent will be treated as having made a gift of a proportion of his business or partnership share and capital transfer tax will be leviable subject to the normal reliefs. To the extent that the child undertakes to devote his full time to the business to relieve the parent of work and to provide for the parent on retirement, the loss to the parent will be diminished and the capital transfer tax burden reduced.

Capital gains tax will also *prima facie* be payable if the child acquires a share in the surplus assets on dissolution either gratuitously or by payment outside the accounts. Since the parties are connected, the parent will be treated as disposing of his interest at market value and capital gains tax will be payable, subject to hold-over relief and retirement relief. If no payment is made by the child and it can be shown that an outsider would have made no payment, the parent will be treated as disposing of the interest acquired by the child at the value of the interest as shown in the accounts (see paras 4, 6 and 7 of the Statement).

If the child simply makes a capital contribution to the partnership and has the right to receive it back, no adverse capital tax consequences arise.

Income tax

It must be remembered that where a child is taken into partnership, for the income tax purposes the business will be treated as coming to an end and immediately recommencing unless all those involved both before and after the change elect, within 2 years, to treat the business as a continuing business (see ICTA 1970, s 154). It will usually be advantageous to elect if the profits of the business are rising.

7.05 Succession to a parent's partnership share

By Will

If a parent by his Will gives his interest in a partnership to a child whether or not the child is already in partnership with the parent, the gift will be subject to capital transfer tax in the normal way; the value of the share will be determined by taking the value of the parent's proportionate interest in the partnership property, including goodwill. By FA 1975, Sched 10, para 9, changes in the value of the parent's estate by reason of death, eg loss of goodwill, will be taken into account. Business property relief will be given and tax will be payable by instalments. Capital gains tax will not be payable and the child will acquire the interest at market value at the date of death.

Automatic accruer clauses

A common provision to be found in a partnership agreement is that on the death or retirement of a partner, his share in the partnership assets shall accrue automatically to the continuing partners. This automatic accruer is usually in return for an annuity for the retired partner or his widow and the reimbursement of his capital contribution.

CAPITAL TRANSFER TAX

If the arrangement is made on arm's length terms with no gratuitous intent, no capital transfer tax arises when the agreement is made nor when the share accrues to the other partners since it then has no value. FA 1975, Sched 10, para 5 may apply and this provides that where the right to dispose of property is excluded or restricted, the exclusion or restriction can only be taken into account subsequently, to the extent that money or money's worth was given for it or to the extent that the agreement for exclusion or restriction was itself a chargeable transfer. Thus, if full consideration is given, no difficulty arises. In *Attorney-General* v *Boden* [1912] 1 KB 539, it was agreed that the father's share in the goodwill of a business should automatically accrue to his sons on the father's death and in return, the sons agreed to devote their full time to the business, not to engage in any other business and that the father should not be bound to give more time and attention to the affairs of the business than he should think fit. It was held that this was full consideration for the accruer. This case only applies to goodwill but there is no reason why it should not apply to all partnership assets particularly if, in addition, an annuity is payable to the retired partner or his widow.

If full consideration in money or money's worth is not given for the accruer, a capital transfer tax charge will arise on the making of the agreement and again, following FA 1975, Sched 10, para 5, when the accruer operates on retirement or death.

The return of the capital contribution will have no capital transfer tax consequence.

CAPITAL GAINS TAX

No capital gains tax will arise when the agreement for the automatic accruer is made. If the accrual occurs on the death of the parent, again, no capital gains tax is payable. If the accrual operates on the retirement of the parent, capital gains tax may apply, and the rules are:

(*a*) since the transaction is between parent and child, ie between connected persons, the parent will be treated as disposing of his share at its market value (the proportionate value of the partnership assets), unless the terms of the arrangement are similar to those which would have been entered into by partners at arm's length, in which case disposal will be at balance sheet values or at the sum actually paid for the share, if any;

(*b*) if an annuity is payable the capitalised value will be treated as a capital sum paid for an interest in the partnership assets unless it is "reasonable", in which case the payment of the annuity will be ignored for capital gains tax purposes. An annuity is regarded by the Inland Revenue as being reasonable if it is no more than two-thirds of the partner's average share of profits in the best 3 of the last 7 years in which he was required to devote substantially the whole of his time to acting as a partner, so long as he was a partner for at least 10 years. If he was a partner for a shorter period of time, the amount of the reasonable annuity is reduced (see para 8 of the Statement).

Options

The partnership agreement may provide that the continuing partners may buy the share of a deceased or retired partner. Usually such an arrangement is fully commercial and the only effect for capital transfer tax is that the option consideration will be the value upon which capital transfer tax is payable if the option is exercised on death. No capital gains tax is then payable. If the option is exercised on retirement, the retiring partner will be treated for capital gains tax as disposing of his share at the option price or, if the option is not for full consideration, at market value. For capital transfer tax purposes, if the option is not granted for full consideration, the same principles apply as for accruer clauses (see above).

7.06 Partnership annuities

The capital gains tax implications of the payment of annuities to a retired partner or his widow have already been noted (automatic accruer, see 7.05). The agreement to pay the annuity will also be part of the consideration for the original partnership agreement which may well mitigate the capital transfer tax consequences. However, the payment of the annuity has further capital transfer tax and income tax implications:

Capital transfer tax

Annuities should not be charged on the partnership assets otherwise unless full consideration is given, the assets will become settled property for capital transfer tax (FA 1975, Sched 5, para 1(2)(*c*)) with serious capital transfer tax disadvantages.

The actual payment of the annuities will give rise to no capital transfer tax if the liability to pay was incurred for full consideration, eg an accruer clause. If the amount of the annuity is excessive a capital transfer tax charge will arise on the payment of the annuity, subject to exemptions. If the widow of a deceased partner is to benefit from an annuity, provided the agreement to pay the annuity was a commercial transaction, there will be no liability to capital transfer tax on the payment of the annuity (see the Inland Revenue Statement in the *Law Society's Gazette*, 2 July 1975 at p 699).

If the transaction is not commercial, presumably the spouse exemption will apply and if the annuity is in favour of others, presumably the exemption for dispositions for the maintenance of the family will apply, if relevant. Otherwise there could be a charge to capital transfer tax on the payment of an annuity to others, if the original transaction was not on commercial terms.

Income tax

THE ANNUITANT

An annuity is investment income taxable under Schedule D Case III but by FA 1974, s 16, in certain circumstances an annuity paid to a retired partner, his widow or dependants, will be treated as earned income up to a limit. That limit is 50 per cent of the average of the partner's share of profits in the best 3 of the last 7 years in which he was in partnership, as increased from 1980/81 by increases in the Retail Price Index. Any balance will be treated as investment income. Retirement must be through age, ill health or death. It will be noticed that the limit is somewhat lower than what the Inland Revenue regard as being reasonable for capital gains tax.

PAYMENT BY THE PARTNERSHIP

Since the annuity is liable to tax under Schedule D Case III in the recipient's hands, it is payable under deduction of basic rate tax under ICTA 1970, ss 52 or 53 (see p 58). Subject to the income tax anti-avoidance provisions, this means that the payment is a charge on income giving full tax relief, although, to the extent that the payment is treated as earned income in the recipient's hands, it cannot reduce the investment income of the payer. Provided no element of bounty exists, the anti-avoidance provisions should not apply (*IRC* v *Plummer*, see p 33); nevertheless ICTA 1970, s 457(1)(*a*) specifically exempts such payments if for full consideration and made under a partnership agreement to or for the benefit of a former partner, his widow or dependants. ICTA 1970, s 457 also exempts payments made for full consideration for the acquisition of a partnership interest. By ICTA 1970, s 457(4), if the right to such payments devolve on the partner's death to a person other than a widow or dependant of that partner, ICTA 1970, s 457 only catches those payments made later than 10 years after the partner ceased to be a member of the partnership.

Consultancies

As an added bonus to a retiring partner, the continuing partners may agree to use him as a consultant and pay him consultancy fees. Such fees will be earned income in his hands but if he fails to carry out a reasonable amount of work in return for the fees, the partners will be given no deduction for the expense.

Since work does have to be done by the retired partner to justify the deductibility of the expense, a consultancy agreement is not usually a suitable alternative to a partnership annuity.

7.07 Partnerships and children: a summary

If a parent is to take his children into partnership as a method of handing down the business to them, the most tax efficient arrangements will be on the following lines.

The child should be given:

(*a*) an interest in the profits of the partnership commensurate with the value of the time, amount of work and experience the child will put into the business;

(*b*) an immediate right to capital which should not exceed any capital contribution made by the child;

(*c*) the right to the automatic accruer of the parent's share on retirement or death of the parent.

In return, the child should agree:

(*a*) to devote his full time to the business and not to act in any other business;

(*b*) to pay a reasonable annuity to the parent, his widow or dependants, on retirement or death;

(*c*) that the parent need devote less time to the partnership business, if appropriate.

Chapter 8

PASSING DOWN THE FAMILY BUSINESS: COMPANIES

8.01 Gifts of shares

This Chapter deals with the particular tax planning problems involved in passing down to successive generations shares in an unquoted family company. The tax planning principles relating to gifts and settlements are dealt with in Chapters 2 and 3 and must be remembered when making gifts of shares. The relevant capital transfer tax and capital gains tax reliefs on the transfer of unquoted shares are set out in Chapter 7 at p 85 *et seq*. These exemptions and reliefs can substantially mitigate the capital tax burden on the gift of shares but it may well be necessary to take further steps to prevent the forced sale of the shares or the liquidation of the company, to pay the tax on a lifetime gift or on death; this Chapter deals with those steps.

8.02 Share valuation

Unlike partnerships where the valuation of a partnership share is basically the value of a relevant proportion of the partnership assets, the valuation of shares in a private company is an art and it is difficult to lay down hard and fast rules. It will always be a matter of negotiation with the Share Valuation Division of the Inland Revenue and the most important way in which the capital tax burden can be mitigated is by negotiating the lowest possible valuation. It is, therefore, essential to take expert advice on the point.

The object of valuation for both capital gains tax and capital transfer tax is to establish the open market value of the shares (CGTA 1979, s 150 and FA 1975, s 38). On lifetime transfers, capital transfer tax is charged on the reduction in the value of the transferor's estate and this involves valuing the estate both before and after the transfer, but the principles set out below still apply.

The valuation of unquoted shares requires a consideration of three factors: the dividend record of the company, its earning capacity and its assets value. Broadly, this works as follows:

Dividend record

Shares can be valued on a dividend basis by taking from the Stock Exchange Lists the dividend yield given by similar quoted companies. A reasonable yield from an unquoted company should be at least 25 per cent more than this, to compensate for the disadvantage of an unquoted holding. The value of the shares can then be ascertained by comparing the yield with the dividend record of the company.

Example
X Ltd has been paying an average gross dividend of £23,000 on its 1,000 shares for the last 3 years and this is likely to be maintained. The average yield of similar companies on the Stock Exchange Lists is 8 per cent. The expected yield from X Ltd is, therefore, 10 per cent, giving a value of the company of £230,000 and a value per share of £230.

Earnings basis

To value shares on an earnings basis, the maintainable profit of the company is calculated and compared with the Price/Earnings ratio given in the Stock Exchange Lists for similar quoted companies. Adjustments may be necessary.

Example
X Ltd has maintainable profits of £100,000 pa. A reasonable Price/Earnings ratio for the type of company is 3. This gives a value of the company of £300,000 and a value per share of £300.

Assets basis

Shares may also be valued on an assets basis, ie as a proportion of the value of the assets of the company, discounted where an individual holding is less than 90 per cent. The discount will be greater for holdings under 75 per cent, ie where no special resolution can be obtained.

Summary

As a rule of thumb, shares will be valued on a dividend basis unless the company is about to be wound-up, when an assets basis valuation will be used. If dividends are low or negligible, a majority holding and perhaps a substantial minority holding (say, above 25 per cent) will be valued on an earnings basis, with a discount for a minority holding. A majority holding may also be valued on an assets basis if that produces a higher figure than the other valuations. With low or negligible dividends, a minority interest under 25 per cent has little more than a speculative value.

These rules will produce different values per share for different sizes of holdings in the same company, particularly because a minority interest has little direct influence on the running of a limited company. This means, for example, that the difference between the value of a 51 per cent holding and a 49 per cent holding can be considerable (see p 104).

For the related property provisions, see p 104.

8.03 Restrictions on the right to transfer shares

The requirement in the Companies Act 1948, s 28 that a private limited company should restrict the right to transfer its shares has been abolished by the Companies Act 1980. However, there will remain a great many companies where the right to transfer shares is restricted and the question is to what extent such a restriction can mitigate the capital tax burden on shares by reducing the value of them.

Examples of restrictions are:

(*a*) that the directors have an absolute discretion to decline to register the transfer of shares (see Companies Act 1948, Table A, Pt II, art 3);

(*b*) that the shares must first be offered to the members of the company and only if they decline to purchase them, can they be sold to an outsider;

(*c*) that the shares can only be sold to members and at a nominal price of, eg £1 per share.

The rule is that restrictions must be ignored when establishing an open market sale and the test is what a hypothetical purchaser would pay for the shares on the assumption he will be registered; that is what would he pay to stand in the transferor's shoes? The price payable may be affected by the restriction since the purchaser himself will then be subject to the restriction, but he will also be influenced, eg by the dividends he is likely to receive. Thus, if shares can only be sold at £1 per share and the unrestricted market value is £10 per share, the actual market value will probably be somewhere between the two (*IRC* v *Crossman* [1937] AC 26).

8.04 Hiving-off

One of the more successful ways of arranging for a business to be passed from parent to child with the minimum capital transfer tax liability, is to arrange for new business opportunities and contracts to be taken on by a new company, the majority of the shares in which are held by or on behalf of the child. The new company can then build up its business over a period of time while that of the old company is run down, thus depreciating the value of its shares. The idea is simple but the process must be gradual and there are problems:

(*a*) it is not possible to transfer capital assets by this method;

(*b*) shareholders in the original company could probably successfully sue any of the directors who were involved in the arrangements, for breach of duty;

(*c*) if any transaction can be identified as having belonged to the original company and as having been taken on by the new company, capital transfer tax could be leviable on the shareholders of the old company (FA 1975, s 39);

(*d*) the value shifting provisions of CGTA 1979, s 26 might be applicable on a subsequent disposal of the shares in the old company, if hiving-off is blatant. This could enable the Inland Revenue to substitute such consideration as the Inspector considers is just and reasonable on a disposal of the old shares, for capital gains tax purposes.

Hiving-off should, therefore, be discreet and should preferably only happen if the business of the original company is to be expanded into another business field or geographical area.

8.05 Share value freezing

The value of shares can be frozen in two ways to avoid tax on increases in value which would otherwise take place:

Rearranging share capital

It is possible to alter the share capital of a company to ensure that any increase in value accrues only to a new class of shares, the existing shares being frozen at their existing value. This is done by issuing a new class of shares which would have rights on the following lines:

(*a*) on winding up, the right to the surplus capital of the company after the existing shares have been repaid their present market value;

(*b*) no right to a dividend initially, but with increasing dividend rights, say after 10 years;

(*c*) no right to vote until, say, 10 years' time.

The issue of the shares could be a bonus issue on renounceable letters of allotment which are then renounced in favour of the child. No stamp duty would be payable.

The problems are:

(*a*) ascertaining and agreeing with the Inland Revenue

the values of the shares can be difficult and time consuming;

(*b*) although the value of the new shares is initially very low, the renouncement in favour of the children will be a reduction in the value of the parent's estate for capital transfer tax and, subject to exemptions and the nil rate band, liable to capital transfer tax;

(*c*) on a subsequent disposal of the old shares, the value shifting provisions of CGTA 1979, s 26 could apply; such a disposal should be avoided.

Granting an option

Share values can also be frozen at their existing value by the grant at full consideration of an option to purchase the shares at present market value. The existence of the option freezes the value of the shares for capital transfer tax on a subsequent lifetime transfer or on death (FA 1975, Sched 10, para 5). If full consideration is not paid, the option will only be taken into account to the extent that consideration in money or money's worth is given for it. The price for such an option is usually around 10 per cent of the current market value of the shares and this can be quite high. Since it is important that full consideration is paid for the option, it may be necessary for the parent to put the beneficiary in funds to purchase the option and this itself may give rise to capital transfer tax.

The option can be granted to the trustees of an accumulation and maintenance settlement for the benefit of the children, or, if they are old enough, to the children themselves. The option can be exercisable for example up to 5 years after the death of the shareholder, so the beneficiary can be put in funds to purchase the shares by a life policy, by a gift by Will or, perhaps, by means of the shareholder's death-in-service benefit from a pension scheme (see p 121).

For capital gains tax the grant of the option will be a disposal of the option (CGTA 1979, s 137) and when the option is exercised, the shares will be disposed of at that time, the grant of the option and its exercise being regarded then as one transaction taking place at the time of exercise. If the option is exercised soon after the death of the shareholder, the capital gains tax base value will, at the date of death, have been uplifted to the option price, so no capital gains tax will arise on the exercise of the option.

8.06 Dividend waivers

Dividend waivers can be useful to increase dividends on the remaining shares in the company, for example those held by children or settlements for the benefit of the children. Following FA 1980 the Inland Revenue no longer have power to apportion the trading income of a trading company, so the payment of dividends will become less common, but if dividends are to be paid, it is more tax efficient to let them accrue to those whose income tax rates are low, including, for example, accumulation and maintenance settlements for children which are taxed at 45 per cent on undistributed income. A dividend received by a child could well be taxed at an overall rate below 30 per cent, because of personal reliefs.

Shareholders who waive dividends must bear in mind the following points:

(*a*) the waiver must be by deed, since it is voluntary;

(*b*) the waiver must take place within 12 months before the right to the dividends accrues so that no capital transfer tax is payable (FA 1976, s 92). The right to a final dividend accrues at the date it is declared by a general meeting. The right to an interim dividend accrues when it becomes payable;

(*c*) if the persons who benefit from the dividend waiver are the infant unmarried children of the person who waives the dividend, it is possible that the Inland Revenue will seek to tax the parent on the increased dividend under ICTA 1970, s 437. If the amount waived accrues to a settlement for the children, ICTA 1970, s 437 will apply to the extent the dividend is distributed or deemed to be distributed.

8.07 Getting over the hump of control

Because of the valuation rules (see 8.02) the difference in value of a controlling holding in a company and a minority interest, can be disproportionately high and, despite the lower capital transfer tax business property relief given to minority holdings – 20 per cent instead of 50 per cent for controlling holdings – it may well be cheaper to give away shares from a minority interest rather than from a controlling interest. It must be stressed that this very much depends on the valuations placed on the shares, but if it is desired to convert a controlling holding into a minority holding, it can be very expensive for capital transfer tax.

Example 1

Shares in X Ltd have been valued as follows:

51% – £150,000
49% – £90,000
2% – £2,000

If the owner of 51 per cent gives away 2 per cent to his child, the value transferred for capital transfer tax is £60,000 (plus tax) less 50 per cent business property relief, since the donor is charged on the loss to his estate. A sale to the child of the 2 per cent interest at £2,000 would probably not be within the non-gratuitous exemption under FA 1975 s 20(4) since it would be very difficult to argue that there is no gratuitous intent and the gift would then be £60,000 – £2,000 = £58,000. If the child paid £60,000 it could be argued that he was making a gift of £58,000 to the parent.

This 2 per cent valuation hump is known as the hump of control and there are two ways round it, using the capital transfer tax related property provisions. These are laid down in FA 1975, Sched 10, para 7 which provides that property comprised in a person's estate is related to other property if that other property is comprised in the estate of a spouse, or is in a settlement with no interest in possession, set up by the transferor or his spouse before 27 March 1974 or it is or has within the last 5 years been the property of a charity. If property is related to other property the value of the property is taken as a proportion of the value of the aggregate of that property and any related property.

Example 2

Husband and wife each own a 26 per cent minority interest in X Ltd. Because of the related property provisions, for capital transfer tax valuation, each will be treated as owning half a 52 per cent controlling holding.

The two schemes are:

1. *Using a spouse*

Taking the figures in Example 1, if a husband owns the

51 per cent interest and gives 2 per cent to his spouse, because the related property provisions will apply, the husband will then be treated as owning 49/51 of the value of a 51 per cent holding, ie his 49 per cent interest will be valued at £144,100 and his wife's 2 per cent interest will be valued at 2/51 of the value of a 51 per cent holding, ie at £5,900. The spouse exemption will apply to the gift. The wife then gives away or sells her 2 per cent interest to the child. She thus loses £5,900 worth of shares, but at the same time the related property provisions cease to apply and the value of the husband's interest drops from £144,100 to £90,000. No capital transfer tax is payable on this drop, since the husband has made no disposition. The associated operations provisions, denying the spouse exemption, should not apply (see Joel Barnett's statement, p 22) but the Inland Revenue might try to argue that the husband has in effect made a gift to the child and should be taxed on the full loss because of FA 1975, s 44.

2. Using a charity

The same principle applies as in scheme 1 above, but instead of using a spouse, a charity can be substituted. The principle was illustrated with a lease and reversion scheme (see p 20). The transferor should give his 2 per cent interest to a charity set up for the purpose. The gift is exempt, but the related property provisions apply. The charity can later sell on the shares to the child. The shares remain related to the shares in the transferor's estate for a further 5 years whereupon he is treated as owning a minority interest only.

Chapter 9

GIFTS ON DEATH

9.01 Generally

Wills

Those who have gone through the conscious process of making a Will should at the same time have considered their overall estate planning position and in particular whether it is appropriate or desirable to make lifetime gifts to their children or issue. If a family business is involved, as has been seen in Chapters 7 and 8, it is usually very important from a tax point of view to take early steps to mitigate the ultimate bill when the business passes to the next generation. In other cases there are a number of factors which will influence a taxpayer in his decision on when and how his children should receive the property he intends them to inherit; this is dealt with in Chapters 2 and 3. When a Will comes into effect on the death of the testator, it should therefore be the final link in the estate planning chain. When making a Will, then, the question is how the estate which you intend should pass on your death should be given to your beneficiaries and what the tax implications are of the dispositions you decide upon.

Family considerations are paramount. A wife will usually outlive her husband, so he must first ensure that she is properly provided for. Since a Will should be made on the basis of a death within the foreseeable future, eg 5 years, this may well mean that the bulk, if not all, of the estate must be bequeathed to a young wife to ensure that she can maintain a reasonable standard of living for the rest of her life. Young children are just as important and provision can be made for them either by ensuring that the wife has sufficient to look after them or by creating a Will trust for their benefit. As will be seen, this latter alternative is usually more tax efficient since it allocates assets to the children.

Intestacies

It is highly unlikely that anyone who dies intestate has put his mind to tax planning, but those who inherit under the intestacy rules will be just as concerned about tax as those who inherit under a Will, so the tax implications of the intestacy rules are considered below.

It must be emphasised that it is never satisfactory to die intestate even if the intestacy rules make the same dispositions as those the taxpayer intended to make anyway. There are many reasons why a Will is to be preferred. For example, it enables the testator to choose who is to look after his estate and the trusts that arise under the Will; guardians can be chosen, and the restrictive investment powers of the Trustee Investments Act 1961 can be avoided. In any event, it is highly unlikely that the dispositions made by the intestacy rules will be satisfactory, except in the case of the very smallest estates, and a Will is necessary to avoid them.

9.02 Benefiting the surviving spouse

How much?

The first question the testator must ask himself is how much he wants his spouse to have, having regard to family matters. No hard and fast rules can be laid down, since it all depends on what the testator wishes and this will be influenced by the age and resources of the surviving spouse, the number and age of the children and any others with a claim on the testator's benevolence and the size and nature of the estate to be given away. As a very rough indication, however, if the estate is small (eg, under £100,000), and the surviving spouse is no more than middle aged and without substantial resources, the whole of the estate should be given to her.

Outright gift or life interest?

Should the gift be outright or should the surviving spouse be given a life interest in the property? A life interest confers only the right to the income from the property given and thus takes away from the surviving spouse the freedom to deal with the property as she wishes. Many testators prefer to give a life interest but couple it with a power enabling the trustees to hand over capital as and when they think fit, and write a letter of wishes addressed to the trustees telling them in what circumstances the testator would like the trustees to exercise that power. Since the surviving spouse will have the income only, it may well be necessary to put into the trust for her benefit more than the testator would give her outright. The spouse exemption applies to both types of benefit.

Minimising capital transfer tax

The next question the testator must ask himself, particularly if there are children or issue, is can the gift by will to the surviving spouse be varied to minimise the overall capital transfer tax bill on the death of both husband and wife? Although a gift to a surviving spouse is generally exempt from capital transfer tax (FA 1975, Sched 6, para 1), because the rates of tax increase progressively the overall capital transfer tax burden is usually greater if all the property of the first spouse is given to the surviving spouse. For example, if each spouse has an estate of £50,000 and has made no lifetime transfers, and the first to die gives his estate to the second, no capital transfer tax is payable then. When the second dies with an estate now of £100,000 the tax bill will be £19,000. If instead the first to die gave the £50,000 to the children, on his death there would be no capital transfer tax since the first £50,000 of chargeable transfers are taxed at a nil rate. On the death of the survivor with an estate of £50,000, no capital transfer tax would be payable for the same reason, saving £19,000. The spouses have, in fact, equalised their chargeable estates. However, it may be undesirable to leave a surviving spouse with £50,000 only.

Should estates be equalised?

It is usually said that the least capital transfer tax arises if the spouses equalise their estates so that on death, each has a chargeable estate (including lifetime chargeable transfers) of the same amount.

Example
H, who dies first, has an estate of £200,000 and has made no previous chargeable transfers. W has an estate of £50,000 and has already made chargeable transfers of £10,000 (taxed at a nil rate). They have two children whom they wish ultimately to take their joint estates. Equalising chargeable estates means that each should have a total of £130,000 of chargeable transfers (half of £200,000, £50,000 and £10,000). This means H must give W £70,000 only and £130,000 to the children. W's estate will then be £120,000 and her total chargeable transfers, including the £10,000 gift, will on her death be £130,000 also.
Contrast this with the tax bill which arises if H gives all his property to W:

	Equalisation	All to W
	£	£
Estate of H	200,000	200,000
Gift to W	70,000	200,000
Chargeable	130,000	nil
Capital transfer tax on death	33,500	nil
Estate of W	120,000	250,000
Lifetime transfers	10,000	10,000
Capital transfer tax on death	33,500	110,000
Total tax burden on both deaths	67,000	110,000
Saving	43,000	

This big saving may be illusory because £33,500 tax has to be found on the first death. The loss of use of this money could be a serious setback if W survives for any appreciable period of time and can also diminish the real value of the saving. Factors such as inflation and changes in the capital transfer tax rates will also affect the overall saving.

Equalisation of estates may well be undesirable therefore and as a rule of thumb, the longer the surviving spouse is likely to survive (bearing in mind that the Will is made on the assumption that the testator will die in the next five years), the less desirable it is actually to pay capital transfer tax on the death of the first.

9.03 Benefiting the children

Having set aside the right amount for the surviving spouse in accordance with the above principles, the balance of an estate will usually be allocated to children with a substitutional provision for issue. It will be inappropriate to make outright gifts to young children and it may be advisable to settle the property for a child of whatever age. The trusts used should be accumulation and maintenance trusts or fixed interest trusts. These are dealt with comprehensively in Chapter 3.

9.04 Which property should the beneficiaries be given?

To minimise capital transfer tax on death (as for lifetime transfers) best use must be made of the exemptions and reliefs available. If property enjoys a capital transfer tax relief or if it is exempt, clearly it should not be given to an exempt beneficiary such as a spouse - the relief or exemption would simply be wasted. For example, property enjoying agricultural relief or business property relief should be given to the children rather than to the surviving spouse.

A lump sum death in service benefit (see 9.09 below) payable under an exempt approved pension scheme will be free of capital transfer tax if payable at the discretion of the pension fund trustees. It is normal practice for the member of such a scheme to indicate in a letter of wishes to the trustees who the member would like to receive the lump sum and the trustees usually respect these wishes. If the testator's remaining estate is sufficient for the surviving spouse, it is a waste of the capital transfer tax exemption to ask the trustees of the pension fund to pay the benefit to the surviving spouse and, furthermore, on her death, what remains of it will be liable to capital transfer tax. Whenever possible, it should be given to the children or, if appropriate, to a trust for the benefit of the children. The trust can be set up by the will.

For the same reason, life assurance policies on the life of the deceased should be taken out for the benefit of the children rather than the surviving spouse; they do not suffer capital transfer tax on the death of the life assured.

9.05 Apportioning values: FA 1975, Sched 6 Part III

The Problem

It is a fundamental principle of capital transfer tax that the amount of a gift includes the tax on it, and if a lifetime gift does not bear its own tax, it is grossed up to find out the amount upon which tax is charged. On death, there is no need to gross up an estate as such, since tax is payable out of the estate. If the testator gives tax free legacies (ie, tax is payable out of the residue) and gives all or part of the residue to an exempt beneficiary the tax on the legacies cannot be paid out of the exempt slice of residue because this would, in effect, partially exempt the legacies. That part of the residue out of which the tax on the legacies is paid must itself be chargeable since it is part of the legacies. Hence it is necessary to gross up chargeable legacies which do not bear their own tax where the estate is partially exempt, to ascertain the true value of the legacies and to ensure that the exemption applies only to property actually passing to an exempt beneficiary. The rules and calculations are laid down in FA 1975, Sched 6 Part III, as amended, and apply, for example, whenever a spouse and children benefit from an estate, unless the gifts to the children bear their own tax.

What gifts bear their own tax?

A gift bears its own tax for the purposes of FA 1975, Sched 6 Part III if the tax attributable to it falls on the person who becomes entitled to the property given or is payable out of property applicable for the purposes for which the property given becomes applicable. The Will will usually be quite clear about which gifts do bear their own tax and which are tax free but, in the absence of a direction in the Will, it would appear that a gift bears its own tax if an Inland Revenue charge is imposed on it by FA 1975, Sched 4 para 20. On death a charge is imposed on all property in the estate except personal or movable property situated in the United Kingdom, such as chattels, leaseholds and undivided shares in land held on trust for sale.

Calculations where all chargeable gifts are tax free non-residuary gifts

The tax free gifts are grossed up normally at the death rates (see table below) taking into account lifetime chargeable transfers. The balance remaining is exempt.

Example

A dies leaving a tax free legacy of £50,000 to his son and the residue of his £200,000 estate to his wife. He made no chargeable lifetime gifts. The legacy must be grossed up, but since it is within the nil rate band, the gross is the same as the net. £150,000 is therefore exempt and £50,000 chargeable and no capital transfer tax is payable.

If A had made £50,000 of chargeable lifetime transfers, the £50,000 legacy would have to be grossed up, producing a figure of £87,777. Thus £112,223 only of the estate is exempt, £87,777 chargeable with tax of £37,777 payable.

Grossing up table

The grossing up table below gives the figures needed to gross up at the death rates of capital transfer tax, using the following method:

1 Take the total of gross *lifetime* chargeable transfers (if nil, go straight to 3).

2 Convert this into a net sum, ie:
   (*a*) take the nearest figure arithmetically in Col 1,
   (*b*) multiply the difference between the two figures by the fraction in Col 3 and
   (*c*) add the result to the net figure in Col 2 adjacent to the figure selected in (*a*).

3 Add to the figure from 2(*c*) the amount of the gifts to be grossed up.

4 Convert this into a gross sum, ie:
   (*a*) take the nearest figure arithmetically below in Col 2,
   (*b*) multiply the difference between the two figures by the fraction in Col 4 and
   (*c*) add the result to the gross figure in Col 1 adjacent to the figure selected in (*a*).

5 The gross figure is obtained by subtracting the figure in 1 from the figure in 4.

Col 1 Gross	Col 2 Net	Col 3 Fraction	Col 4 Fraction
50,000	50,000	7/10	10/7
60,000	57,000	13/20	20/13
70,000	63,500	3/5	5/3
90,000	75,500	11/20	20/11
110,000	86,500	1/2	2
130,000	96,500	9/20	20/9
160,000	110,000	2/5	5/2
510,000	250,000	7/20	20/7
1,010,000	425,000	3/10	10/3
2,010,000	725,000	1/4	4

Example

Gross up tax free legacies of £100,000. The testator has made previous lifetime chargeable transfers of £75,000.

1 Gross lifetime transfers are £75,000.

2 Convert this into a net sum, ie:
  (*a*) take £70,000,
  (*b*) multiply £75,000 – £70,000 = £5,000 by 3/5 = £3,000 and
  (*c*) add this to £63,500 = £66,500.

3 Add to £66,500 the £100,000 legacies = £166,500.

4 Convert this into a gross sum, ie:
  (*a*) take £110,000,
  (*b*) the difference is £166,500 – £110,000 = £56,500; multiply by 5/2 = £141,250 and
  (*c*) add this to £160,000 = £301,250;

5 thus the grossed up amount of £100,000 is £301,250 – £75,000 = £226,250.

It will readily be appreciated that this grossing up can eliminate residue in some cases.

Calculations where some chargeable gifts are tax free but others (eg residue) bear their own tax

To find the gross chargeable legacies in these circumstances needs more complex calculations, and FA 1975, Sched 6 Part III requires the grossing up to be done in an artificial manner, as follows:

1 Gross-up all the tax free chargeable gifts as if they were the only chargeable gifts (use the grossing-up table above).

2 Add the actual amount of the other chargeable gifts. This produces a "hypothetical" value transferred.

3 Calculate the amount of capital transfer tax on this value transferred without grossing-up. This pro-

duces an "assumed amount of tax".

4 Calculate the rate of tax produced by the assumed amount of tax on the hypothetical value transferred. The rate produced is known as the "assumed rate".

5 Gross-up tax free chargeable gifts at the assumed rate and this produces the gross value to be attributed to them. Remaining gifts are attributed with their actual values or, in the case of residue, with what is left after these calculations.

6 Calculate capital transfer tax using these attributed values.

Example

A dies leaving an estate of £200,000. He gives tax free legacies of £30,000 to each of his two sons and the residue of his estate is given to his wife and daughter in equal shares. The calculations are:

1 Tax free legacies total £60,000 (the chargeable share of residue bears its own tax). The gross of this is £64,615.

2 The other chargeable gift is the half share of residue. The amount is, for these purposes, half of £200,000 − £64,615 = $\frac{135{,}385}{2}$ = £67,692·50. The hypothetical value transferred is therefore £64,615 + £67,692·50 = £132,307·50.

3 The assumed amount of tax, ie tax on £132,307·50, is £34,769 (no grossing-up).

4 The assumed rate is $\frac{£34{,}769}{£132{,}307\cdot 50}$ = 26·28 per cent.

5 Gross up £60,000 at 26·28 per cent, ie $\frac{£60{,}000}{100-26\cdot 28} \times 100$ = £81,388.

Gross values to be attributed to the gifts are therefore:

Legacy to first son	£40,694
Legacy to second son	£40,694
Residue is £200,000 − £81,388 =	£118,612
Daughter's share is	£59,306
Exempt share to widow is	£59,306

Thus the transfer is chargeable as to £81,388 in legacies and £59,306 residuary share, a total of £140,694.

6 Tax on £140,694 is £39,381 giving an estate rate of 27·99 per cent. The distribution is:

(*a*) The two sons receive £30,000 each. Tax to be paid out of residue is on £81,388 (attributed value) at the estate rate of 27·99 per cent = £22,781.

(*b*) Residue is £200,000 − £60,000 = £140,000 less the tax of £22,781 payable on the legacies = £117,219. The daughter's chargeable share is £58,609·50 and bears tax at 27·99 per cent on the *attributed value* of £59,306 = £16,600. The daughter therefore actually receives £58,609·50 − £16,600 = £42,099·50. The wife receives £58,609·50.

Tax planning conclusions

It will have been noticed that, in the example above, the gross sum attributed to the legacies to the sons is less than that required to produce net legacies of £60,000 (the attributed gross value is £81,388 and tax is £22,781). If the legacies had been expressed as a gross figure, which after bearing tax produced £60,000, that gross figure would have been greater, increasing the chargeable estate and thus the tax bill.

The rule is, therefore, that tax is saved (although the amount saved is not great) if legacies are made tax free where residue is partly exempt or where residue is wholly exempt and other non-exempt gifts are made which do bear their own tax. There is *never* a disadvantage in making legacies tax free (except in the complexity of the calculations!).

9.06 Post mortem tax planning

It sometimes comes as an unpleasant surprise when a testator is told that what he puts in his will can often quite easily be rearranged by his beneficiaries after his death, for example by mutual agreement, by disclaimer, by assignment of the benefit or by the beneficiary himself making a gift of the benefits given to him by the Will (or intestacy). Minor children beneficiaries cannot indulge in such rearrangements to their detriment without Court consent, but there is no objection to increasing their benefit.

It may come as a ruder shock to the testator that the capital taxes legislation actively encourages such rearrangements. On basic principles the rearrangement would be a disposition reducing the value of the estate of the person whose benefit diminishes for capital transfer tax, and for capital gains tax a disposal of property at market value. However FA 1978, ss 52 and 68 (now CGTA 1979, s 49) respectively enable those concerned to relate the rearrangement back to the date of death and treat it as if it had been made by the deceased himself both for capital transfer tax and capital gains tax.

For capital transfer tax, FA 1978, s 68 provides that a consideration free written variation of the dispositions of a deceased's estate or a disclaimer of a benefit under the will or intestacy made within two years after the death, takes effect as if made by the deceased at the date of death, provided written notice is given to the Board of the Inland Revenue within six months after the variation or disclaimer. A separate but similar right is given by CGTA 1979, s 49 for capital gains tax.

The possibilities can be seen in the following example:

Example

A dies leaving all his £200,000 estate to his wife. He had made no chargeable lifetime transfers. His widow wants their children to receive £50,000 from his estate and within two years after his death she varies the will to this effect. If she gives written notice to the Revenue within six months thereafter, the rearrangement, which is effectively a gift of £50,000 by her to her children, is treated as being part of her husband's dispositions, ie he is deemed to have given £50,000 to his children and £150,000 to his widow. No capital transfer tax is payable since the chargeable gift to the children is within A's nil rate band.

If the widow makes the rearrangement but fails to give the notice, it will be treated as a gift of £50,000 by her to her children. Again, no capital transfer tax is leviable as the gift is within the widow's nil rate band. Having regard to the equalisation of estates above, depending on the size of the widow's own estate, it may be more tax efficient to give the notice.

If, on the other hand, A had already made chargeable lifetime gifts of £100,000, when the rearrangement is made if the widow elects to treat the gift as having been made by A (subject to tax), the tax bill on A's death on the £50,000 would be £17,500. If the gift to the children is treated as being tax free, using FA 1975, Sched 6 Part III (as shown above), the tax bill would be an enormous £62,500. On the other hand, if the widow fails to give notice, the £50,000 gift will be made by her and no capital transfer tax will be payable.

Clearly, FA 1978, s 68 and CGTA 1979, s 49 should be used to ensure that the deceased uses up his nil rate band of capital transfer tax, but whether it should be used further remains a matter of judgement.

Similar provisions apply where property is left on precatory trusts and the legatee acts in accordance with the testator's wishes. This allows for flexibility where the testator trusts the principal beneficiary. For example, a testator may leave his personal chattels to his solicitor absolutely and express the wish that his solicitor should distribute them in accordance with written or oral instructions given by the testator, or otherwise to be distributed amongst the testator's children at the solicitor's-discretion. This creates no legal obligation on the solicitor, who becomes the beneficial owner of the property. However, when he distributes in accordance with the testator's wishes within two years after the death, FA 1975, s 47(1B) automatically treats the dispositions as having been made by the testator rather than the solicitor.

FA 1975, s 47(1A) gives relief for capital distributions out of the testator's discretionary settlement. This gives further scope for tax avoidance on death and is dealt with below.

9.07 Using discretionary trusts for flexibility in a Will

New discretionary trusts generally suffer serious capital transfer tax drawbacks and, unless they are accumulation and maintenance trusts, a Will should not usually contain discretionary trusts. However, there is scope for maintaining great flexibility in a Will by using discretionary trusts and making use of FA 1975, s 47(1A). This provides that where the Will sets up a settlement with no interest in possession and within two years after the date of death a chargeable event occurs, such as the distribution of trust assets or the creation of a fixed interest settlement or an accumulation and maintenance settlement, the chargeable event is not itself taxable but is deemed to have been part of the dispositions made by the deceased's Will. In other words, the chargeable event is related back to death.

When making his Will, a testator cannot know what circumstances will be prevailing after his death; he cannot know who will then be in need, what his property will be worth nor what the capital tax position will be then. If he can trust his executors implicitly (particularly their judgment), he can leave all or part of his property on pure discretionary trusts and leave it to the executors to distribute as they think fit within two years after his death. Unlike precatory trusts, the discretionary trusts are legally binding on the executors.

This avoids difficulty where minor children are involved. Minor children cannot be parties to rearrangements of an estate and discretionary trusts ensure that they have no say in the matter!

Drafting of such trusts requires care, and capital transfer tax will arise if the executors fail to act within the two year period, so it is advisable to provide that after, eg twenty-three months, the discretionary trusts shall terminate and alternative dispositions made by the testator shall come into effect; these alternative dispositions will also, by FA 1975, s 47(1A), be automatically related back to the death.

9.08 The intestacy rules

Succession by spouse and issue

Where an intestate dies leaving spouse and issue, or just minor issue, trusts arise. For the surviving spouse the trusts are fixed interest trusts; for minor issue they are accumulation and maintenance trusts. It is therefore of fundamental importance to know what are the terms of these trusts and their tax implications.

By AEA 1925, s 46, where an intestate dies leaving a spouse and issue, his estate must be distributed as follows:

(*a*) personal chattels to the spouse;

(*b*) a statutory legacy of £25,000 to the spouse, plus 7 per cent interest from the date of death to the date of payment; and

(*c*) the remainder of the property to be held as to one half for the spouse for life with remainder to the issue of the intestate on the statutory trusts and, as to the other half, for the issue on the statutory trusts.

Where the intestate leaves issue but no surviving spouse, the whole of the intestate's estate is held for the issue on the statutory trusts. The intestate's property is held on a statutory trust for sale (AEA 1925, s 33) and the personal representatives' power of investment is restricted to the powers given by the Trustee Investments Act 1961 (AEA 1925, s 33(3)) but they do have the powers of maintenance and advancement under TA 1925, s 31 (see p 39) and s 32. Section 32 empowers the trustees of a settlement to advance up to one-half of a beneficiary's presumptive share in capital (vested or contingent). Consent of any beneficiary with a prior interest is required.

The spouse's trusts

The life interest of the spouse is an interest in

possession for capital transfer tax and the capital transfer tax and capital gains tax implications are covered at pp 47–49; the interest given will be covered by the spouse exemption. Three particular points should be noted, however.

(*a*) by AEA 1925, s 47A the spouse has the right to elect within twelve months after the personal representatives obtain a grant to the estate, to capitalise the value of the life interest, ie to take the capital value of the right to the income for the rest of her life. The method of calculating this value is laid down in s 47A and obviously produces a smaller sum than the half share of residue in which the life interest subsisted. The effect of capitalisation is twofold:

(i) it is for capital transfer tax purposes related back to death (FA 1975, s 47(3)) and the intestate is thus treated as giving his surviving spouse the smaller capital sum, thus increasing the potential capital transfer tax bill, and

(ii) the issue's interest in the balance of the half share of residue is accelerated and is deemed to have been given to them at the date of death together with the other half share which is already held for them on the statutory trusts.

(*b*) If the surviving spouse does not elect to capitalise her life interest and subsequently during her lifetime it is thought desirable to advance some of the capital of her fund to the children, eg under TA 1925, s 32 or, where relevant, by the surviving spouse releasing part of her life interest, capital transfer tax will be levied on the surviving spouse as if she had made a gift of the capital advanced or released. At the same time, for capital gains tax her interest comes to an end and the children become absolutely entitled, so by CGTA 1979, s 54 the trustees will be deemed to dispose of the property involved at market value and immediately reacquire it and capital gains tax may be payable. If the property advanced or released is instead then held on trust for the children, the capital gains tax charge would arise under CGTA 1979, s 55;

(*c*) the charge to capital transfer tax will not arise if the intestate died during the era of estate duty, provided the trust fund bore estate duty on the death of the intestate since the limited interest of surviving spouse exemption will then apply (FA 1975, s 22(4)).

The statutory trusts for children

AEA 1925, s 47 sets out the statutory trusts for issue on intestacy. The property is to be held on trust in equal shares for those of the intestate's children living at the date of his death who attain the age of eighteen or earlier marry. If any child predeceases the intestate leaving issue living at the intestate's death, such issue take their deceased parents' share *per stirpes* and in equal shares between them. No issue can take if their parent is living at the intestate's death and so capable of taking.

On reaching eighteen, therefore, or on earlier marriage, beneficiaries become absolutely entitled to the capital of their share. Until then, TA 1925, s 31 (power of maintenance) applies and, as has been seen on p 39, this makes the trusts, accumulation and maintenance trusts for capital transfer tax, so no capital transfer tax arises when a beneficiary becomes entitled to capital. It is possible that if the right to the property vests on the beneficiary's marriage under the age of eighteen, no capital gains tax is payable under CGTA 1979, s 54 (see p 45).

So far as the half-share in which the surviving spouse has a life interest is concerned, the children or issue only have reversionary interests and take when the surviving spouse dies. This reversionary interest is, for capital transfer tax, excluded property and the beneficiaries can give it away, eg to their own children, without capital transfer tax and capital gains tax.

It can be seen that one of the major disadvantages of the intestacy rules is that children become entitled at the age of eighteen or earlier marriage. Many parents prefer to postpone a child's inheritance until more mature years. To do this requires a Will.

9.09 Pension fund benefits for children

Employee pension schemes

Pension fund benefits given to employees are central to tax planning for children, because of the substantial benefits which can be given to the children without liability to capital transfer tax. A pension fund itself is one of the most tax efficient vehicles for investment that exists, if it is an exempt approved scheme (as most are), since contributions by the employer and the employee are tax deductible and the fund itself is income tax and capital gains tax free. Furthermore, contributions by an employer are not taxed as benefits in kind under Schedule E in the employee's hands.

The benefits payable under such a fund include:

(*a*) For the employee, a pension of ⅔ final pensionable salary after ten years' service. This is taxed as earned income under Schedule E.

(*b*) The employee may commute part of this to realise a tax free lump sum for himself of up to 1½ times his final pensionable salary after twenty years' service.

(*c*) A tax free lump sum payment of up to four times his salary can be made if the employee dies in service. If this is payable to those in whose favour the trustees exercise their discretion, it is not liable to capital transfer tax. The employee is at liberty to write to the trustees telling them who he would like to benefit from the payment and they will generally respect his wishes. As has already been noted (p 111), this is a very substantial tax free benefit and should usually be paid to children rather than a surviving spouse, to prevent duplication of exemptions.

(*d*) A widow's pension of ⅔ the employee's pension.

(*e*) A dependant's pension in addition to a widow's pension on the death of the employee, provided that they do not together exceed what the employee's pension would have been, or was.

None of these benefits give rise to a charge to capital transfer tax at any stage (except where a lump sum forms part of a deceased's estate at death) and every taxpayer who can, ought seriously to consider becoming a member of his employer's pension scheme.

Pension schemes for the self-employed

The self-employed can be worse off than the employed when it comes to pensions. The method of providing pension benefits is by way of retirement annuities, taxed as earned income, but there are restrictions on funding which do not exist in employee pension schemes, and which can reduce the benefits payable.

The maximum contribution a self-employed person can

make to such a scheme is 17½ per cent of net relevant earnings (basically all taxable earnings without deduction) and, of that, only 5 per cent can be put to funding an annuity for widow, dependants and death in service benefit. It is simply the funding which keeps the size of the benefits down. The member is himself entitled to commute part of his pension to realise a capital sum, but the amount of this sum is restricted to three times the annual amount of the pension which remains after payment of the lump sum.

Benefits are still capital transfer tax free and should therefore be directed in the same way as for the employee.

Index